JEAN ANOUILH

WORLD DRAMATISTS

JEAN

ANOUILH

LEWIS W. FALB

WITH HALFTONE ILLUSTRATIONS

FREDERICK UNGAR PUBLISHING CO.

NEW YORK

Copyright © 1977 *by Frederick Ungar Publishing Co., Inc.*
Printed in the United States of America
Designed by Edith Fowler

Library of Congress Cataloging in Publication Data
Falb, Lewis W
  Jean Anouilh.

  (World dramatists)
  Bibliography: p.
  Includes index.
  1. Anouilh, Jean, 1910–   —Criticism and
interpretation.
PQ2601.N67Z58   842'.9'14   72-79928
ISBN 0-8044-2189-7

CONTENTS

CHRONOLOGY

1910   Jean Anouilh is born on June 23, near Bordeaux.

1918–29   Anouilh's primary and secondary education is in Paris; he studies law briefly at the Université de Paris.

1929–31   Anouilh works as a copy writer for an advertising agency, and also as a "gag" writer for the movies.

1931   Anouilh marries the actress Monelle Valentin.

1931–32   Anouilh works as secretary to Louis Jouvet at the Comédie des Champs Élysées.

1932   Anouilh writes *Jézabel*, which is not performed. *L'hermine* is staged at the Théâtre de l'Œuvre, April 26, directed by Paulette Pax. Anouilh decides to devote himself exclusively to the theater.

1933   *La mandarine* is staged at the Théâtre de l'Athénée, January 16, directed by Gérard Bothedat.

1935   *Y avait un prisonnier* is staged at the Théâtre des Ambassadeurs, March 21; film rights are sold to Metro-Goldwyn-Mayer.

1937   Anouilh meets two directors who are to have

major influences on his career: Georges Pitoëff and André Barsacq.

Le voyageur sans bagage is staged at the Théâtre des Mathurins, February 16, directed by Georges Pitoëff.

1938   *La sauvage* is staged at the Théâtre des Mathurins, January 10, directed by Georges Pitoëff. *Le bal des voleurs* is staged at the Théâtre des Arts, September 17, directed by André Barsacq.

1940   *Léocadia* is staged at the Théâtre de la Michodière, November 28, directed by Pierre Fresnay.

1941   *Le rendez-vous de Senlis* is staged at the Théâtre de l'Atelier, January 30, directed by André Barsacq.

1942   *Eurydice* is staged at the Théâtre de l'Atelier, December 18, directed by André Barsacq.

1944   *Antigone* is staged at the Théâtre de l'Atelier, February 4, directed by André Barsacq.

1946   *Roméo et Jeannette* is staged at the Théâtre de l'Atelier, December 3, directed by André Barsacq.

1947   *L'invitation au château* is staged at the Théâtre de l'Atelier, November 4, directed by André Barsacq.

1948   *Ardèle; ou, La marguerite* is staged at the Comédie des Champs Élysées, November 3, directed by André Barsacq. *Episode de la vie d'un auteur* is staged at the Comédie des Champs Élysées, November 3, directed by André Barsacq.

1950   *La répétition; ou, L'amour puni* is staged at the Théâtre Marigny, October 25, directed by Jean-Louis Barrault.

1951   *Colombe* is staged at the Théâtre de l'Atelier, February 11, directed by André Barsacq.

1952   *La valse des toréadors* is staged at the Comédie des Champs Élysées, January 9, directed by Roland Piétri.

Anouilh publishes *Trois comédies de Shakespeare* (adaptations of *As You Like It*, *Twelfth Night*, and *The Winter's Tale*).

1953   Anouilh marries the actress Charlotte Chardon. *L'alouette* is staged at the Théâtre Montparnasse–Gaston Baty, October 14, directed by Jean Anouilh and Roland Piétri.
Médée is staged at the Théâtre de l'Atelier, March 26, directed by André Barsacq.
Anouilh adapts, with Paule de Beaumont, Eugene O'Neill's *Desire under the Elms*, which is staged at the Comédie des Champs Élysées, November 5.

1954   *Cécile; ou, L'école des pères* is staged at the Comédie des Champs Élysées, October 29, directed by Roland Piétri.
Anouilh adapts, with Claude Vincent, Oscar Wilde's *The Importance of Being Earnest*, which is staged at the Comédie des Champs Élysées, October 29.

1955   *Ornifle; ou, Le courant d'air* is staged at the Comédie des Champs Élysées, November 7, directed by Jean-Denis Malclès.

1956   *Pauvre Bitos; ou, Le dîner de têtes* is staged at the Théâtre Montparnasse–Gaston Baty, October 11, directed by Roland Piétri.

1957   Anouilh adapts, with Claude Vincent, William Shakespeare's *Twelfth Night*, staged at the Festival de Toulon.

1959   *L'hurluberlu; ou, Le réactionnaire amoureux* is staged at the Comédie des Champs Élysées, February 5, directed by Roland Piétri.
La petite Molière is staged at Bordeaux, June 1, and later at the Odéon–Théâtre de France, November 12, directed by Jean-Louis Barrault.
Becket; ou, L'honneur de Dieu is staged at the Théâtre Montparnasse–Gaston Baty, October 8, directed by Jean Anouilh and Roland Piétri.

1960   Anouilh produces Molière's *Tartuffe* at the Comédie des Champs Élysées, November 5.

Le songe du critique is staged at the Comédie des Champs Élysées, November 5, directed by Jean Anouilh.

1961   Anouilh, with his daughter Nicole, does another adaptation of Shakespeare's *Twelfth Night*, which is staged at the Théâtre du Vieux Colombier, February 28.

La grotte is staged at the Théâtre Montparnasse–Gaston Baty, October 4, directed by Jean Anouilh and Roland Piétri.

1962   *La foire d'empoigne* is staged at the Comédie des Champs Élysées, January 11, directed by Jean Anouilh and Roland Piétri.

L'orchestre is staged at the Comédie des Champs Élysées, January 11, directed by Jean Anouilh and Roland Piétri.

Anouilh produces Roger Vitrac's *Victor; ou, Les enfants au pouvoir* at the Théâtre de l'Ambigu, October 3.

Anouilh adapts, with Nicole Anouilh, Graham Greene's *The Complacent Lover*, which is staged at the Comédie des Champs Élysées, November 11.

1964   Anouilh adapts William Shakespeare's *Richard III*, which is staged at the Théâtre Montparnasse–Gaston Baty.

1966   Anouilh adapts Heinrich von Kleist's *Das Kätchen von Heilbronn*, which is staged at the Théâtre Montparnasse–Gaston Baty, October 20.

1968   *Le boulanger, la boulangère, et le petit mitron* is staged at the Comédie des Champs Élysées, November 13, directed by Jean Anouilh and Roland Piétri.

1969   *Cher Antoine; ou, L'amour raté* is staged at the

Comédie des Champs Élysées, October 1, directed by Jean Anouilh and Roland Piétri.

1970   *Les poissons rouges; ou, Mon père, ce héros* is staged at the Théâtre de l'Œuvre, January 21, directed by Jean Anouilh and Roland Piétri.

Ne réveillez pas madame is staged at the Comédie des Champs Élysées, October 21, directed by Jean Anouilh and Roland Piétri.

1971   *Becket* enters the repertory of the Comédie Française in October.

1972   *Tu étais si gentil quand tu étais petit* is staged at the Théâtre Antoine, January 17, directed by Jean Anouilh and Roland Piétri.

Le directeur de l'Opéra is staged at the Comédie des Champs Élysées, October 27, directed by Jean Anouilh and Roland Piétri.

1974   *Monsieur Barnett* is staged at Le Fanal, Café-Théâtre des Halles, October 29, directed by Nicole Anouilh.

1975   *L'arrestation* is staged at the Théâtre de l'Athénée, September 20, directed by Jean Anouilh and Roland Piétri.

1976   *Le scénario* is staged at the Théâtre de l'Œuvre, October 1, directed by Jean Anouilh and Roland Piétri.

Chers zoiseaux is staged at the Comédie des Champs Élysées, December 3, directed by Jean Anouilh and Roland Piétri.

A COMIC MISANTHROPE

> It would be possible to write two parallel biogra-
> phies of an author, one of the ordinary life he
> leads, the other of his secret life, of his creative
> sensitivity, which also has a childhood, an adoles-
> cence, and a maturity that bear no resemblance to
> his own childhood, adolescence, and maturity.[1]

Taking Anouilh's own words as a guide, I think it
appropriate to consider only those aspects of his life
that relate directly to his career as playwright, thereby
respecting his deep-seated desire for privacy. Indeed,
Anouilh has often insisted that he has no biography at
all, and as a result of his reticence we know very little
about the details of his personal life. In addition—and
more important—Anouilh feels that the creative and
intellectual career rather than the historical facts of a
writer's life constitutes the true biography, for that is
"perhaps one's real life."[2]

Anouilh's earliest education in the theater was a
thorough grounding in turn-of-the-century operetta and
light comedy. His mother was a pianist, and for a time

she played in the theater orchestra of the Casino in Bordeaux. In the evenings young Jean was permitted to watch the performances. This early contact with the theater provided him with a rich source of images and themes. The language, the atmosphere, the characters of the world of the theater, especially of second-rate theater, left an indelible impression on him.

Anouilh has written that he learned by heart the songs and the situations of the plays he saw. But since, as a young boy of eight or nine, he had to leave at intermission, he never found out how these works ended. As a result, his inventive mind fashioned its own solutions and dénouements for these complicated and fanciful plots. The world he saw on stage became his book of fairy tales, his book of legends. He himself claims: "The basis of my theater is there. You can find in it the comic and the trivial, the 'heavy' and the young male lead. I have remained at the level of the theater of my childhood."[3]

From his father Anouilh acquired an appreciation of craft, a respect for work carefully done. Anouilh *père* was not a dramatist; he was a tailor. Nevertheless, it was he who taught his son the "feeling of a professional conscience and the nobility it gives to a man."[4] Anouilh has explained: "I write plays because that is all I know how to do, and I write them the way my father used to cut his suits."[5]

After an uneventful formal education, including the study of law for a brief time, Anouilh took a job as a copy writer in an advertising agency. This experience was particularly useful in the formation of the playwright:

> I learned lessons of precision and ingenuity there that have taken the place for me of the study of

poetry. Even now I constantly get good ideas for publicity. Moreover, a slogan presupposes a precision of words within a phrase that resembles the strictness necessary for lines in a play. A line is effective because of its precise structure. Change it, and it becomes ineffective.[6]

Anouilh's commitment to the theater was encouraged by Georges Neveux, a playwright and fellow copywriter who introduced him to Louis Jouvet, one of the most important *metteurs en scène* (producer-director) in Paris. Jouvet hired the young writer as his secretary. This opportunity enabled the fledgling dramatist to make contact with the professional theater and with one of its ablest talents.

Anouilh and Jouvet were, however, very different. "I was very pure at thirty," Anouilh has said. "Lack of compromise was something important to me."[7] Jouvet was older and more used to the necessities and realities of the world. When Anouilh showed him his work, Jouvet was not very encouraging. Some time later Anouilh took one of his plays, *Le voyageur sans bagage*, to Georges Pitoëff, and Jouvet never forgave Anouilh for this. The two *metteurs en scène* were at opposite poles of theatrical technique. Jouvet, famous for his elaborate productions, for his elegance and taste, was contemptuous of the spare stagings of the Pitoëffs; he called Georges and his actress-wife Ludmilla *les pitoyables*.

Although Pitoëff presented only two of Anouilh's works—*Le voyageur sans bagage* and *La sauvage*—the young playwright was deeply influenced by the simplicity and purity of Pitoëff's approach. Anouilh still feels "filial gratitude" toward the "only true genius"[8] he met in his life. Pitoëff's style became Anouilh's ideal—a theater in which the settings, the stage properties, all the physical aspects of mounting a work were secondary. Everything in Pitoëff's productions was stripped to the essentials: his was a theater in which the play of the mind, of the intellect, was the prime interest.

In 1932 Anouilh, at the age of twenty-two, decided to support himself exclusively by writing for the theater or films. Since then almost all aspects of his life seem to be completely bound up with the stage: life and art, the world outside the playhouse and the world inside it, have meshed for him. The frequently repeated anecdote about the young Anouilh and his first wife, the actress Monelle Valentin, living in an apartment furnished with parts of the set for Jean Giraudoux's *Siegfried*, which Jouvet had lent the young couple, offers an apt symbol for the intensity of this commitment. After his divorce Anouilh again married an actress, Charlotte Chardon. Indeed, all the women in his life, including his daughters, are involved with the theater. Catherine has had success as an actress, while Nicole has worked with her father on the adaptations of several plays and has directed one of his recent works, *Monsieur Barnett*.

There was, however, at least one event with no immediate or direct connection to the theater that Anouilh frequently refers to. This event represented a brusque awakening to political and social realities. Completely involved in his own writing, Anouilh was naïve about worldly issues during and immediately following the Nazi Occupation of France. When he learned that Robert Brasillach, a novelist and fellow dramatist, had been condemned to death for collaborating with the Germans, Anouilh tried to collect signatures from writers and intellectuals in an attempt to save him. Setting out full of enthusiasm and idealism, Anouilh returned from his quest an "old man, as in one of the Grimm fairy tales."[9] His failure to acquire more than seven signatures, his contact with a world he had not known before, instilled doubt, distrust, misanthropy—the word is not too strong—which have never left him:

> It is from this time and from the years that fol-lowed that my precise knowledge of the scenario and its pitiful characters date. . . . The story is not great. These rather theatrical tricks, this ridicu-lous melodrama, this sinister buffoonery, these half-comic traitors, reeking of convention, with their uniforms, their Legions of Honor, their glory, their big words, this was really what it was; this was life.[10]

He has not abandoned this vision of life and human-ity. His profound opposition to De Gaulle, his seeking "refuge" in Switzerland in 1946, his artistic silence be-tween 1962 and 1968, his refusal to let his work be performed in "official" theaters while *le Général* was in power—all these political responses date from the period of that first disillusionment. Nevertheless, Anouilh is not really a political person; he rejects all political solu-tions: "I have no political thoughts. My refusals are those worthy of a concierge; they are instinctive."[11]

Anouilh has revealed little else about his life not directly involved with his writing. In this area, however, he has been quite explicit and generous, openly acknowl-edging his debts to other writers. In many ways Anouilh is the most typical French dramatist of the century, almost as if he alone, in his own oeuvre, were attempt-ing to encapsulate the development of the drama in twentieth-century France.

Anouilh's early work, influenced by realism and naturalism, presented somber studies of sordidness and compromise. This mode was not entirely satisfying to him, and in a very short time, following the examples of other writers, Anouilh broke with this style and never returned to it. He profited from the efforts of Giraudoux, of Jean Cocteau, and perhaps of Paul Claudel, to free the theater from realism. He also learned from the surrealist experiments of Roger Vitrac. These influences have been tempered, however, by Anouilh's admiration for classical French theater—chiefly his devotion to Molière—and also by the effect the works of the Italian dramatist Luigi Pirandello had on him.

The first major influence on Anouilh's theatrical development came in the spring of 1928, when he saw Giraudoux's *Siegfried* as staged by Jouvet at the Comédie des Champs Élysées. It revealed to Anouilh a poetic theater in which he found the embodiment of all he wanted to do. Through Giraudoux, Anouilh claims to have discovered the "theater, my life in beauty . . . poetry, all that was inaccessible."[12] Seeing *Siegfried*—three times—was both inspiring and depressing for Anouilh; he was delighted at having discovered this nonrealistic, poetic theater; but he was distraught at realizing that all he might seek to accomplish would seem feeble by comparison.

From Giraudoux Anouilh adopted the notion that one of the basic aspects of theater was to be "real," to tell the truth, within a framework of unreality. Picasso's epigram, "Art is a lie that makes us realize truth," succinctly describes this approach. Giraudoux's method deliberately stresses theatricality. He calls attention to the actual fact of theatrical performance through his extraordinarily rich language, and his use of monologues, set pieces, and debates. The writing is intended to strike the spectator not as an imitation of everyday life but rather as a reminder of the conventions of theater itself. The larger-than-life heroes of Giraudoux, idealized and exceptional, are also intended to transport the members of the audience from day-to-day concerns to a plane on which they can confront more complex and timeless truths.

The second of Anouilh's important early contacts with a concept of drama beyond the limits of realism was his reading of Cocteau's *Les mariés de la Tour Eiffel*. Cocteau was attempting to write plays in which all forms of theatrical expression would have a place. His goal was to achieve a poetic theater not by writing verse drama but by employing music, dance, costumes, even pantomime to give the most banal and ordinary situations a poetic quality, to portray scenes from everyday life in a new perspective. Cocteau's play was a revelation to Anouilh:

> From the very first line something melted in me, a huge block of transparent ice that was barring my way. Everything fell into place. . . . Jean Cocteau had just given me a sumptuous and frivolous gift; he had just given me the "poetry of the theater."[13]

In the works of Claudel, Anouilh found yet another example of poetic drama, of an anti-naturalistic theater in which an imaginary universe, the sole creation of a poet, is to be accepted as the "real" world. Here was a spiritual writer who had developed a theatrical mode that freed the author from the confines of realism and extended the range of his expression.

From Vitrac's experimental theater, Anouilh learned how to modulate farce into serious drama. In Vitrac's best-known play, *Victor; ou, Les enfants au pouvoir*, the setting is the familiar environment of commercial or Boulevard theater, a recognizable world in which the

spectator feels quite at home. But while using traditional theatrical devices, Vitrac prepares to explode
this comfortable and predictable order to reveal the
corruption at the heart of a base and ignoble society.
For Vitrac, humor must not mask the basic seriousness
of the content. While we laugh at the vitality, the
freshness, the bawdiness of *Victor*, we do not lose sight
of its brutality. The play is, according to Anouilh,
"very good Feydeau, written in collaboration with
Strindberg."[14] In 1962 Anouilh staged an important
revival of *Victor*.

The most important foreign influence on Anouilh's
style was Pirandello's work. From the "old Sicilian
magician,"[15] Anouilh learned lessons in dramatic technique, especially the interchangeability of the "real"
and the "unreal," of truth and illusion. And he has
acknowledged this great debt: "I am a descendant of
Pirandello, that's all. *Six Characters*, I haven't invented
a thing since."[16]

Anouilh has carefully studied Pirandello's "theater"
plays—*Six Characters in Search of an Author, Tonight
We Improvise*, and *Each in His Own Way*. Of *Six
Characters in Search of an Author*, for example, Anouilh
has said "theater changed that day. It was he who
invented the idea of destroying an anecdote and playing with it."[17] It should be noted, however, that
Anouilh's familiarity with the works of Pirandello and
with their effectiveness on stage confirmed rather than
initiated the direction in which his own instincts and
talent were moving.

These twentieth-century playwrights all contributed
importantly to Anouilh's development, but the playwright who has dominated his vision of theater, who
has most decisively shaped Anouilh's conception of

comedy, is the seventeenth-century genius Molière. "When you find a true comic writer in France," Anouilh has said, "you always must go back to the patron saint."[18] For Anouilh, Molière "wrote, in the form of reasonable comedy, the blackest theater in all of literature."[19] It is exactly this combination that occurs in Anouilh's theater. Indeed, Anouilh finds a similarity between Molière's age and ours:

> The seventeenth century was a black century. It had its abysses, but it did not show them off complacently to visitors. . . . It built above them a structure of convention, as harmonious and as consciously false as possible.[20]

For Anouilh, Molière provides truer insight into the human condition than all the fashionably despairing descriptions of man's nothingness being written today, for Molière did not lose sight of the fact that man is both pitiful and comic:

> We can wound each other, betray each other, kill each other using more or less noble pretexts. We can puff ourselves up with supposed grandeur, but we are comic. And nothing else—each as much as the other, including those whom we call heroes.[21]

This quality of laughter, derived from understanding and insight, gives special distinction to the work of Molière:

> Thanks to Molière, the true French theater is the only one in which one does not say Mass, but in which one laughs—like men at war, their feet in the mud, hot soup in the stomachs, their weapons in hand—at our misery and at our horror.[22]

The result of so many influences on Anouilh is a body of work that is both typical and distinctive. The basis of Anouilh's dramaturgy is the idea that theater must "create by every artifice possible something truer than truth."[23] For him, this has meant the invention of devices and gimmicks designed to call attention to the artificiality of the presentation. Instead of trying to hide the strings on his puppetlike figures, he often does his utmost to make us aware of them. And the facile jokes and implausible situations recur not, as he claims, because he cannot resist the temptation but rather because they are an integral part of his intention. Moreover, Anouilh has been attracted more and more to the theater as the very setting of his plays. The world of theater is not only the perfect image of an artificial creation designed to reveal the truth; it is also the representation for Anouilh of life as it is. The decors with which we surround ourselves are not much more stable than that which we see when the curtain goes up. The frantic and frenzied activity of the farces we witness during some theatrical performances is the very image of our lives:

> These games of illusion, these confusions, these unexpected exits and entrances with which you have come to amuse yourself, thinking that by paying your way in you have protected yourself—what if this were also *your* life?[24]

Theater for Anouilh is also a prime necessity, not only for himself, but for all men:

> It is a religious thing, and man needs, from time to time, to get together with other men to witness

that fiction which is played before him on a stage
as if it were the truth, played for him alone.[25]

Anouilh is acutely aware of the essential seriousness
and, indeed, nobility of his profession. His concept of
his role as a writer takes him far beyond his frequent
pose as a popular entertainer. He seeks a balance between farce and high seriousness—a very delicate balance that he succeeds in maintaining in his best work
with almost breathtaking skill. Anouilh writes about the
instability of social institutions, the absurdity of most
human activity, and the frightening emptiness of most
men's lives—themes that are the common currency of
twentieth-century literature. But unlike many of his
contemporaries, these themes are treated in such a way
as to appeal to a wide and diversified audience. He has
managed to do what few postwar playwrights in any
country have done—to bridge popular and serious
theater.

In addition, his work is infused with the rare quality
of genuine compassion. As one character in his play
Cher Antoine says, "Have you noticed that it is the
cynic who is most often moved to tears?" Anouilh's
flawed, often ridiculous and bumbling protagonists
strive to preserve some vestige of integrity. And their
struggle, although doomed to failure, becomes a profoundly touching and accessible image of man's worth.
The sharpness of Anouilh's sardonic vision makes his
final compassionate conclusion the more effective.

In the more than forty years since his first play was
staged in Paris, Anouilh has worked with very few
directors; as is traditional in French theater, he col-
laborates closely with the man responsible for the play's
physical production, the *metteur en scène*. Perhaps the

most famous twentieth-century example of such an alliance is the Louis Jouvet–Jean Giraudoux partnership; almost all of Giraudoux's plays were directed by Jouvet and performed by his company. This cooperation, one can almost say co-creation, was a model for Anouilh, who was, after all, Jouvet's secretary for a time. As his own career became established, Anouilh, too, actively involved himself in the staging of his work.

Between 1938 and 1953, Anouilh's principal director was André Barsacq, who presented nine of his plays at the Théâtre de l'Atelier: *Le bal des voleurs, Léocadia, Le rendez-vous de Senlis, Eurydice, Antigone, Roméo et Jeannette, L'invitation au château, Colombe,* and *Médée.* Gradually, however, Anouilh began to feel the need to have much more direct (and finally complete) control:

> I left Barsacq because to whisper into someone's ear every five minutes, "It would be better to do it this way," is not the same thing as to take charge and say, "No, this is how it's done," and explain directly to the actors.[26]

With the exception of two plays mounted by Jean-Louis Barrault—*La répétition* and *La petite Molière*—and one by his daughter Nicole—*Monsieur Barnett*—all of Anouilh's premières in recent years have been directed by Anouilh himself, or by Roland Piétri in collaboration with Anouilh. In addition, since 1948, almost all of Anouilh's plays have been designed by Jean-Denis Malclès. This continuity is not accidental but indicative of Anouilh's constant and meticulous attention to every aspect of his work. As a result of this "team" creation, there is a distinctive appearance, a recognizable "look," to an Anouilh play: the techniques of design and the style of direction are constants. Indeed, Anouilh even prefers to use the same actors from one play to another, thereby creating his own small acting company. For example, Michel Bouquet, who played the Dauphin in *L'alouette*, also had the title role in *Pauvre Bitos* and appeared as Adolphe in *Le boulanger, la boulangère et le petit mitron*. And Paul Meurisse, who created the protagonist of *L'hurluberlu*, was also the two historical rulers—Napoleon and Louis XVIII—in *La foire d'empoigne*. The secondary characters in his plays, types who reappear from work to work, are also often played by the same performers. This enables Anouilh to write with certain actors in mind, something that some of the great dramatists—like Shakespeare and Molière—seem to have found congenial. The effect of all this is to guarantee in performance the kind of theatricalism Anouilh seeks in his writing. Audiences are attending an Anouilh play that shares features with all other Anouilh plays. It can never be mistaken for transposed life. It is artificial but true to itself.

In the study of Anouilh's development over a forty-year period and in almost as many works, it is convenient to begin with the classifications the author himself has devised for the volumes of his collected plays. Anouilh's descriptive titles do have limitations. These categories should not be expected to signify a rigorous system. In fact, the first two, the *pièces noires* and the *pièces roses*, were improvised at the time of publication. Moreover, as one will discover in the following chapters, the best play of each group—the one I have singled out for discussion at length—is in some cases precisely the one that least conforms to the category in which it is placed. Nevertheless, Anouilh's descriptive titles suggest for each group a common period of creation, as well as some thematic and stylistic unity. Taken broadly, the categories can be a useful starting point for appreciating the variety and richness of Anouilh's writing.

THE PLAYS

Le voyageur sans bagage
and the *Pièces noires*

A harsh and brutal world, uncompromisingly bleak, together with a starkly naturalistic style, characterizes those of Anouilh's earliest plays known as the *pièces noires*. These plays—*L'hermine, La sauvage, Le voyageur sans bagage*, and *Eurydice*—present the first statements of Anouilh's recurrent theme of the individual's futile and painful attempt to survive in a hostile environment. On the whole, these plays are rather simple and naïve, not quite in the melodramatic realm of the good guys fighting the bad, but not at too far a remove. The conflict is between innocent youth and corrupt society, between the present and the burden of the past. The struggle of the young is almost always doomed to failure and, accordingly, the dominant mood of these works is bitter and cynical; the playwright is often, in fact, brutal and strident. Indeed, Anouilh recently said that he has some difficulty in rereading these works of his youth: "I get the impression that I am reading plays by my son—a young man who isn't me."[1]

Since the subject matter as well as the tonality of

these plays is firmly rooted in the traditions of natural-istic theater, passion and murder are common. But jealousy, incest, and greed are presented in such over-stated terms in the two earliest of these plays, *L'hermine* and *La sauvage*, that one's credulity is strained. Only in the two later plays—*Le voyageur sans bagage* and *Eurydice*—does Anouilh begin to modify his melo-dramatic material by theatricalizing it.

L'hermine (1932), the earliest of the *pièces noires*, is a mixture of romantic comedy, detective story, and social drama. The protagonist is a poor young man obsessed by what he feels to be the dishonoring and corrupting effects of poverty. He kills his fiancée's wealthy aunt so that the young woman can inherit enough money to ensure their happiness. But only after he confesses his crime to the police does his fiancée once more tell him she loves him. Such a synopsis reveals the play's melodramatic outline. And, in truth, the issues are so simply drawn, right and wrong are so sharply and exaggeratedly presented, that it is difficult to respond to *L'hermine*. But the emo-tional intensity in the handling of Frantz's poverty and his preoccupation with purity suggests that these sub-jects were close to Anouilh's own struggles during the early years of his career. These give the work a measure of sincerity that tempers some of the sensationalism.

La sauvage (1938) traces a young woman's struggles against the influences of her family and her past. When Thérèse falls in love with a wealthy young man, far removed from her sordid life, she finds she cannot accept the happiness he offers; she cannot reject what has been so much a part of her. Moreover, she cannot accept happiness itself while others continue to suffer. In this work Anouilh presents without violence the conflict between what he calls the "two races," the haves and have-nots. As background, the shoddy café orchestra in which the heroine and her family perform is appropriately sordid and unpleasant, but the play does not overemphasize the brutal and the crude. It is worth noting that this orchestra, a pitiful caricature of the world of art, is to appear repeatedly in Anouilh's writing.

One must simply suppose that nonliterary demands, perhaps some publishing exigencies, caused the inclusion of *Eurydice* (1942) among the *pièces noires*. It is not quite at home here for it shares neither chronology nor theme with them. And stylistically, *Eurydice* anticipates the *nouvelles pièces noires,* for it is Anouilh's first attempt to retell a classical myth. This Orpheus and Eurydice are a typical pair of young Anouilh lovers: he is a struggling violinist playing in cafés and spas; she is an actress in a second-rate touring company. In some of its minor details the play resembles the original myth, and Anouilh's treatment is theatrically effective. But Anouilh seems clumsy or uncomfortable in superimposing the legend on his own familiar world. For example, when Eurydice returns from the dead, surely the heart of the myth, Anouilh's adherence to the legend requires an almost arbitrary imposition of events. That his Orpheus deliberately looks at Eurydice out of love, to spare her future corruption, is a common Anouilh motivation, believable and moving. But that Eurydice should have come back from the dead in the first place is now improbable. It is here only because it is required by the myth. Anouilh's spectator is left confused and unconvinced, and his response to the work is accordingly reduced.

Le voyageur sans bagage (1937), like *L'hermine* and *La sauvage,* deals with the subjects and themes of

naturalistic drama, but here Anouilh boldly and imagin-
atively alters his approach. Rather than present his
plays as a slice of life, he introduces anti-naturalistic
elements to heighten the theatrical nature of the work.
What results is an unlikely marriage—a philosophical
meditation cast as a comedy.

The first scene of the play is set in the living room of
a wealthy provincial family, the Renauds. At the rise
of the curtain the maître d'hôtel ushers in the Duchess
Dupont-Dufort, her lawyer, and a young man named
Gaston. During the long expository opening scene we
learn that Gaston is an amnesiac who has spent the
eighteen years since World War I in an asylum. The
Duchess, a meddling old woman, has been trying to
rediscover his family and his past. They have come to
the house of the Renaud family to continue their
search. The mood of these opening moments is light
but brittle. The foolish and fanciful Duchess, with her
excesses of imagination, belongs in the salons of
drawing-room comedy. Gradually, however, she reveals
her prejudices, her snobbery, and her rigid sense of class
distinctions. These are not comic. Her shallowness and
hardness sharply contrast with the initial impression
she creates. Such an unexpected combination is typical
of Anouilh's method in this play.

The Renauds—Madame Renaud; her elder son,
Georges; and his wife, Valentine—now enter, eager to
learn if Gaston is indeed a member of their family.
Gaston has gone into the garden while the Duchess
tries to prepare them for possible disappointment; they
are, after all, one of five families still seeking to claim
Gaston. When he finally reenters, Madame Renaud
exclaims that he is indeed her missing son Jacques.
Gaston looks at each of them very carefully and stops
briefly in front of Valentine. She whispers, "My dar-

ling," but Gaston turns to the Duchess and, shrugging almost apologetically, says, "I am really sorry," as the curtain falls.

In the following scene, set in the hallway outside the living room, the servants take turns peeking through the keyhole and commenting on what they see. While giving additional information about the Renaud family, the servants' reactions also provide a comic refraction, undercutting the rather melodramatic story. Through the servants we learn that Jacques was, in the words of the chauffeur, a "little bastard" whose presumed death was no loss to anyone. Furthermore, some sinister hints about his character suggest that Jacques was malicious, not simply spoiled or thoughtless.

The third scene takes place in Jacques's bedroom. Madame Renaud and Georges are showing Gaston around the house in hope that something will awaken his memory, but Gaston claims that nothing is familiar to him. Gaston has, in fact, created for himself a wistful fantasy of an innocent and ideal past, and everything he hears about Jacques contrasts sharply with this. Jacques, for example, took great pleasure in killing birds and small animals; the best specimens were even stuffed and placed in his bedroom. And although both Madame Renaud and Georges at first deny that Jacques ever had a special boyhood comrade, when pressed they finally admit that at seventeen Jacques had paralyzed his best friend in a fight. For the full details of this incident Gaston insists on talking to Juliette, the maid who had witnessed the accident. Left alone with Gaston, she confesses that she and Jacques had had an affair. His quarrel with Marcel was caused by Jacques's jealous outburst when he caught his friend kissing Juliette. In the fight Marcel was thrown down a flight of stairs. Gaston is horrified not only at this story but also at the maid's attitude: she is still delighted to have had two young men quarrel over her. Her admiration for Jacques precludes any moral judgment.

To Georges, with whom Gaston is next alone, he expresses amazement at the general lack of indignation over Jacques's crime; Georges, too, it seems, can excuse Jacques. Georges claims that Jacques's behavior was merely a "childish act, a sinister childish act." Gradually Georges discloses further crimes in Jacques's past. At one time Jacques had swindled half a million francs from an old friend of the family. But what strikes Gaston as Jacques's worst offense is that he was Valentine's lover. This, too, Georges seems somehow to have accepted: Jacques "was hard, yes, inconsiderate, fickle. But I loved him with all his faults." Gaston, however, reacts with indignation, calling Jacques a bastard when he learns of his betrayal of his brother.

Madame Renaud, the next to have a private talk with Gaston, is shown to be a cold and stubborn woman. Her relationship with Jacques was constantly strained; indeed, in the year before he entered the army, they had not spoken to each other, for she had refused to allow Jacques to marry the young seamstress he was in love with. Gaston is repelled at the thought of a mother who would allow her son to go off to war without a word of tenderness. As Gaston repeats Jacques's phrase, "I hate you," the two men seem to merge for a brief moment. But once again Gaston insists he is not Jacques and rejects "this devouring thing which you call a past."

Now it is Valentine's turn to try to "reclaim" Jacques. She is the first of those young women frequently encountered in Anouilh's plays who sells herself in marriage. At one time she had been Jacques's girl friend, but family pressures forced her to marry his older brother. It is soon obvious that she is an unsentimental, clear-thinking, and resourceful young woman who without apparent difficulty or suffering has adjusted to the terms life has imposed. She now insists that Gaston do the same: "You are going to become a man again, with all that this entails of stains, of erasures, and also of happiness. Accept yourself, and accept me."

Valentine had already proven her tenacity by bribing her way into Gaston's asylum some time ago and making love with him (although he had not recognized her), demonstrating that the crimes of the past rather frighteningly do not remain only in the past. If Gaston is indeed Jacques, he will have to deal with a crime, even if unwittingly committed, that is not imputable simply to the errors of youth.

Their scene is comically interrupted by the Duchess and the *maître d'hôtel*, who enter in a state of consternation. The other families claiming Gaston have unexpectedly arrived. When these two go off to arrange things, Valentine offers Gaston final, irrefutable proof of his identity. As the curtain falls she tells him of a scar unknown to anyone else, which she made by jabbing a hat pin in his back when she thought he had been unfaithful.

Following this rather melodramatic revelation, Anouilh, in the brief fourth scene, uses the material to good dramatic effect. Two of the servants are peering into Gaston's room through the transom. They cannot understand why he has removed his clothes now or, what is more, why he begins to weep after examining himself in a mirror. Their comments, comic and vulgar, act as a filter, a commentary on what might have been an unbelievable moment, as Gaston discovers that he can no longer hide the feared truth from himself.

The fifth and final scene again takes place in

Jacques's room. It is morning and the Duchess and Madame Renaud enter with the *maître d'hôtel*. Hoping to startle the sleeping Gaston into regaining his memory, they quietly arrange the room with the stuffed birds and animals that Jacques as a child had taken such delight in killing. When Gaston awakens, he is indeed startled by the trophies around him, but gradually we see him moved to sorrow and guilt by these victims of his past.

Georges enters and tries to make Gaston realize that Jacques was not solely responsible for his monstrous behavior; his family shared much of the blame. He was a spoiled child who could not handle the money they so lavishly thrust upon him. Too young to deal with the hardness and coldness of his mother, too weak to turn out well without a strong masculine influence, Jacques should not be judged too severely. In Georges's words, "In spite of all you have been told, don't hate him too much, this Jacques. . . . I think he was, above all, a poor kid."

Gaston is now determined to reject his past. His deliberation is played out against comic counterpoints while Gaston is getting dressed with the help of the *maître d'hôtel*. When Gaston wonders aloud if he has the right to "kill" Jacques, the *maître d'hôtel* takes him literally and thinks him both mad and violent. Thus, Anouilh makes us laugh at the servant while we watch Gaston reach a decision of the gravest importance.

Valentine enters after the *maître d'hôtel* has fled in comic terror. Gaston, jubilant that he is now sufficiently sure of himself to be able to refuse his past, the people in it, and even himself, says to her: "I am probably the only man to whom destiny has given the possibility of realizing this universal dream. . . . I am a man, but

I can, if I want to, be as new as a child." This per-
ception is an illusion, however, for Valentine reminds
Gaston that if he refuses the Renaud family he will
simply have to accept another—and who knows what
crimes, what horrors, await him. Anouilh seems to be
implying that the life of Jacques Renaud was, in fact,
not exceptional. And Gaston learns that there is no
escape; there is no way of freeing oneself from society
or the family.

Gaston is totally defeated, trapped. Even returning
to the asylum is impossible; as he has acknowledged,
life there was filled with the most menial tasks and
hampered by the most prisonlike controls. Valentine
has stripped him of even the slightest shred of hope.
When she leaves, Gaston, catching a glimpse of himself in a mirror, hurls an object at his reflection, to
destroy, at least symbolically, what he sees there. Then,
melodramatically, he collapses on the bed, his head in
his hands.

At this moment Anouilh provides a striking theatrical effect. The curtain does not fall, as we might have
expected; instead we hear music, at first sad, then, according to the stage directions, "in spite of Gaston, in
spite of us, more lively." A young boy enters dressed in
an Eton suit. One of those seeking to claim Gaston, he
is the lone survivor of the English branch of the family,
and by a strange and farcical turn of events, the uncle
of the missing man. If he and his guardian Mr. Pickwick do not find this missing nephew, he will lose his
inheritance. Here at last is the answer to Gaston's
problem. He will save both the boy and himself. Rejecting the Renaud family's claim, Gaston informs the
Duchess that he plans to live with his seven-year-old
uncle and Mr. Pickwick in a "very beautiful house in

Sussex with wonderful ponies." And on this happy ending, accompanied by appropriately triumphant music, the curtain descends.

With this final scene Anouilh mocks his audience's desire for a happy ending. The blatant improbability of this charming conclusion serves to emphasize the fantasy. Life, unfortunately, is not like this: we know that Gaston's story would have had an unhappy conclusion. The obvious artificiality of Anouilh's comic resolution makes us aware of the impossible dilemma of his hero. Like us, Gaston cannot escape his past, eliminate the influences of his family, and ignore the demands of society. Like ours, Gaston's desire for purity, innocence, and absolute integrity cannot withstand the constraints and requirements of the world in which we must live.

Thus, Anouilh's deliberately contrived ending is not, as some have suggested, merely a self-indulgent dramatic trick, nor is it faulty craftsmanship. Anouilh realized that the naturalistic and realistic modes had become so commonplace that French audiences would have been uninterested and unmoved by a straightforward presentation of Gaston's story. Nevertheless, Anouilh seems to have wanted to maintain at least a link with the naturalistic tradition, because its vision of the corruptibility of man, a vision that prevails in the work of late-nineteenth century writers like Zola, provides the basis of the philosophical structure of this play. *Le voyageur sans bagage* is an unsparing expression of the cruelty, greed, and pettiness Anouilh finds in man.

In his earlier *pièces noires* Anouilh sought to present his view of the human condition directly. In doing this, he risked writing melodrama. But in *Le voyageur sans bagage* Anouilh combines a melodramatic action with comedy and fantasy. The result is both more ironic and

more forceful. Anouilh learned elements of this approach from such directors as Louis Jouvet and Georges
Pitoëff late in the 1930s, and from the example of such
playwrights as Giraudoux, Cocteau, and Pirandello.
Through them, Anouilh was introduced to the possibilities offered by a heightened theatricality. In this
work he explores for the first time what was to become
a hallmark of his dramatic method.

Early in *Le voyageur sans bagage* the Duchess, somewhat melodramatically, feels herself caught up in a
conflict of great dimensions—and she is not wrong.
Gaston is indeed involved in a "merciless struggle
against fate, against death, against the obscure forces
of the world." The question he poses throughout the
play is the very basis of all morality: How is one to
live? Standing apart from the world, Gaston can see
the choices and compromises lying ahead of him. He
realizes that coldness, hardness, and indifference will
necessarily follow his reentry into the everyday world.
His vision of life is bleak and despairing, for Gaston—
and probably his creator as well—perceives it as a process of gradual erosion, of the destruction of the individual physically and, more importantly, morally. Once
one becomes a part of the world, once one steps over
the threshold and leaves the asylum, once one reaches
adulthood, the process of contamination is inevitable:
there is no hope of escape. In the real world, alas, there
is no Uncle Madensale in an Eton suit, no lovely
houses in Sussex, no wonderful ponies.

Le voyageur sans bagage, which Louis Jouvet had
refused to stage, was first presented by Georges Pitoëff
in February, 1937, at the Théâtre des Mathurins.
Pitoëff himself portrayed the leading role, and his wife,
Ludmilla, appeared as the young English boy in the

final scene. This unusual casting recurs in Anouilh's later works; a young woman plays the important role of Toto in both *Le boulanger, la boulangère et le petit mitron* and *Les poissons rouges*. The French theater, so much freer than American drama from the confining demands of realism, can employ such devices to guarantee the level of performance in important roles.

Pitoëff's production of *Le voyageur sans bagage* was well received. Critics praised the quality of the performances and found that in this work Anouilh, although still perhaps too "literary," had made considerable strides beyond his earlier work. The play was successfully revived in April, 1944, with Pierre Fresnay as Gaston, and again in 1950 with Michel Vitold in the lead. When the play was restaged in October, 1973, by Anouilh's daughter, Nicole, critics found that for the most part it had still not aged; it retained the power, the leanness, the directness of its youth.

In New York *Traveler without Luggage* did not fare well. It opened in September, 1964, with Ben Gazzara and Mildred Dunnock in the main roles and ran for only forty-four performances. John Chapman in the *Daily News* found that the play demonstrated "more intellect than it does emotion, but that is usually the way with Anouilh." Many of the critics failed to recognize that the artificiality of the ending was intentional, and so they spoke of the "uncomfortably contrived ending" (Norman Nadel in the *World Telegram and Sun*).

Le rendez-vous de Senlis
and the *Pièces roses*

The *pièces roses* and the *pièces noires* are opposite sides of the same coin, reflecting only differences of approach and technique. They are inspired by a similar vision of reality and were conceived at the same time. In fact, Anouilh's progression within them is comparable; in both he moves from a rather straightforward presentation in the earlier plays to a richer mixture of tonalities and emotions. The early *pièces roses* are almost pure fantasies, comedies that are ballet-like in their artificiality. Indeed, in their purest form they do not seem to be in harmony with Anouilh's general temperament or outlook:

The dance-like entrances and exits, these multiple plots . . . gave me a terrible time. . . . I still dream at night about all the torment I had, all the insoluble problems that made me spend weeks in front of a blank page. I am delighted to have got out of all that, and I would not start that again for anything in the world.[2]

Anouilh is rather more in his element when he unites the comic and the serious, the fantastic and the real. This he attempts in the most important of the *pièces roses*, *Le rendez-vous de Senlis*. Still, the other three plays in this group—*Humulus le muet*, *Le bal des voleurs*, and *Léocadia*—were, at the least, very useful experiments in the development of the playwright's craft, and they have a unity and coherence lacking in the more ambitious *Le rendez-vous de Senlis*.

Humulus le muet (written 1929) is the earliest of Anouilh's *pièces roses*, and, indeed, of all his published plays. Written when he was nineteen, this brief one-act comedy strikingly foreshadows much of Anouilh's future work. In the play, Humulus, a mute young man, has the power to say a single word a day. To declare his first love, he goes thirty days without speaking to build up his supply of words. But after his impassioned declaration he discovers that his beloved is hard-of-hearing and has missed all he has said. This is a charming fable, and a sad one. The solitude of the protagonist, the difficulty of communication, the bitterness of life's ironies—these themes make this short play, prized by French amateur theatrical groups, a fitting curtain-raiser to Anouilh's theater.

Le bal des voleurs (1938) is a delightful *comédie-ballet*, clever and sophisticated, to be sure, but finally somewhat empty-headed. The plot concerns a trio of professional thieves at work in a fashionable spa, who use a variety of disguises and masquerades to rob a wealthy woman and her nieces. Although at times the play seems to be treating the theme of role-playing and false appearances, illusion and reality, these ideas are only touched on lightly, for farcical action dominates the work. The rapid and headlong rhythm of this divertissement sweeps away any of the serious or somber notes that occasionally appear.

Léocadia (1940), the last of the *pièces roses* to be written, continues to deal in dazzling surfaces and brilliant fantasy. Like *Le bal des voleurs*, *Léocadia* raises questions of illusion and reality in such a way as to leave the audience amused but untroubled. The play revolves around a young prince's desire to re-create the brief idyll he had with Léocadia, a famous singer, now dead. The innocence, simplicity, and directness of the young girl hired to impersonate Léocadia win out over the extravagance, complexity, and oddity of Léocadia herself; the "real" world triumphs over the fantasy world. This very elaborate and stylized fairy tale has all the enchantment of wish fulfillment, but not very much of the ring of truth.

In *Le rendez-vous de Senlis* (1941), written before *Léocadia* but staged the year after, Anouilh had tried for something more substantial by blending the themes and vision of tragedy with the form and techniques of comedy. Although this play deals with two worlds— the somber and bitter world of everyday reality and the optimistic, attractive world of the imagination—Anouilh here stresses that the two worlds cannot be neatly compartmentalized.

At the beginning of *Le rendez-vous de Senlis* we are in the rococo living room of a town house in Senlis (just outside Paris). Georges, the young protagonist, is being shown through the house by the landlady. He has come to Senlis to rent the house for just one night. In the scene with the landlady, and one with a caterer's representative that follows, Georges reveals that the house is intended to represent his parents' home.

Georges, it seems, has told Isabelle, the young and innocent girl with whom he has been having an affair, all about his family, and she is coming to dinner this evening to meet them. The family Georges described, however, does not exist. Georges is thus arranging a very elaborate theatrical performance. And when the *maître d'hôtel* announces Madame de Montalembreuse and Monsieur Philémon, a pair of down-on-their-luck actors, Anouilh puts us squarely in the world of theater.

These actors are a vain pair, rather full of bombastic self-importance, a too-noisy dedication to their art, and a too-grand notion of their talent. When Georges tells them that they are to play his parents, they immediately fall into the clichés of stage parents. The actress imagines herself as a mother still very young and feminine, one who has "remained very much a woman," and the actor sees the father as a doddering old man. Almost apologetically and in sharp contrast to the farcical behavior of the actors, Georges explains that what he is asking is of great importance, despite its ridiculous appearance. His speech goes beyond the particular situation and assumes the seriousness of an *art poétique* for Anouilh:

> You who are used to a theater in which they do not mix the genres must be amazed at this young man who is leading you into vaudeville, with a long face and trembling hands. Other people quite naturally have tragedy at their disposal; at the slightest leave-taking, at the slightest difficulty they can wave their handkerchiefs and let go with their tears, surrounded by universal emotion. It happens that I have to play my life like a comedy, that's all.

The parents Georges describes to the actors are the perfect storybook couple. The father is a charming, youthful man, more of an older brother than a parent. He is stern when necessary, strong and reassuring. When Georges proceeds to describe the mother he has in mind, he enumerates not what she is, but what she is not. She is not the overly good woman of sentimental plays: "they sacrifice themselves too easily and too often." Nor is she the bad one of melodrama, who abandons her child on the church steps; after all, "there are so many simple ways of abandoning a child, even while keeping him at home until he is of age." She is fundamentally the dream mother, the image fantasized by little boys as they stand in the kitchen beside the impatient maid waiting for their mother to come back home "wearing too much perfume, from her eternal errands in the afternoon."

Georges proposes that he and the actress play a brief scene, a rather conventional one: the young son refuses to marry the wealthy young woman his parents have chosen for him because he loves a poor working girl. This scene would seem to be straight out of sentimental drama, but something more is at work here. When Georges speaks his lines, the stage directions indicate that he does so "with his eyes closed, in an odd voice; we no longer know to whom he is speaking."

Georges is delighted with the noble and generous response offered by the actress in her interpretation of the role of Mother. Her understanding, her wish for his happiness, her respect for love, are exactly what the dream mother would have expressed. Then the actress admits that this situation has a parallel in her life. She has a grown son who wanted to marry for love. Unlike the loving mother she has just enacted, however, she forbade her son to marry his "little violinist, a little nothing of a tramp." Instead of understanding, he received a slap on the face. The ambiguities and complexities of the mother-son relationship are here under-scored by the contrast between reality and fantasy.

In this long scene, which dominates the first act, Georges is putting together a performance; he is going to act out his life—or more precisely, his life as he wishes it to be. Although he may have set the stage and sketched the characters, the script is not written, and the actors' independence can lead in unexpected directions.

In the final moments of the first act Georges sketches for the actors a picture of himself as a very sincere, timid, good-natured, somewhat naïve and provincial young man. As the act ends, however, this idealized image is undermined by its being presented amid a rush of accelerated movement and of slapstick gags. The curtain falls as Isabelle arrives for the rendez-vous.

From the rococo salon of the first act we move in the second to the linen room of Georges's Parisian home. From the airy world of comedy of manners and fantasy, we descend into the sordid world of bourgeois drama. In the first act we witness an attempt to create an ideal environment; in the second we encounter reality and discover what, in fact, is motivating the protagonist.

Toward the end of the first act Georges was called off-stage for a telephone call. As the curtain rises on the second we find Barbara—Georges's mistress, we later learn—speaking to him on the telephone. She tells him that his family is in a state of extreme anxiety because his wife, Henriette, has been threatening to throw them all out if Georges does not return at once. From the other members of the family—Georges's real parents and his "best friend"—who all find their way to the linen room, presumably the place where they can escape Henriette's eye, we learn the details of Georges's life. He does not love his wealthy wife, who is tempera-

mental and demanding. Their marriage had been arranged by his parents to help alleviate family financial
problems. The scene between Georges and the actress
in the first act was indeed a moment in Georges's past.
The desire to replay the episode, and perhaps change
the outcome, indicates the extent of frustration and
bitterness in him.

Georges's family is presented as a dismal bunch of
self-centered, scheming hangers-on. They loathe one
another; each is concerned only with maintaining his
own comfort. In this moment of crisis they are revealed
in a particularly harsh and unflattering light. Georges's
real father is cynical and unfeeling; his mother is a
vain, selfish, foolish pleasure-seeker who imagines that
she cannot survive without luxury. She will do anything to hold onto her style of living, even renounce her
son: "I am Georges's mother, granted, but I am, above
all, Henriette's friend." Robert, the best friend, is no
better than the others. He and Georges have been
friends since childhood, and as is typical in Anouilh's
world, they consequently detest each other. Robert
hates Georges because he is better-looking, more clever,
and is his wife Barbara's lover. But above all, Robert
hates Georges because Georges has married a very
wealthy woman and Robert now lives on Georges's
charity. Barbara is the only one who is beginning to
become disgusted with both herself and the group. She
reveals to the others where Georges has gone, and at
the act's end they all run off desperately to Senlis to
find Georges and bring him back.

This second act shows us the cruel reality from which
Georges is trying to escape. This act also adds another
dimension to the portrait of Georges. We now see
three facets: first, the Georges who is a pleasant, con-
trolled, and rather mysterious young man, somewhat

disturbing and rather sad; second, the idealized picture of Georges as he imagines he would like to be; and third, the Georges of the real world as seen by his family, rather weak, self-indulgent, and immoral, in some ways hardly better than the unpleasant people who surround him.

The third act returns to the house in Senlis, and continues the action with the entrance of Isabelle, which had been interrupted by the fall of the first-act curtain. Although intended by Georges to be the setting for a fantasy, the house now serves for a drama very much of this world. The meeting of Isabelle, Georges's young and innocent new love, and his family will now be played, but not in the way Georges had planned.

Isabelle becomes the focal character as she is confronted immediately with the actors Georges had hired; they explain the truth of the situation to her and Isabelle even pays them their fees. Then the members of Georges's real family arrive in Senlis. Of these, Isabelle first meets Robert, who enters before the others. This scene humanizes the almost caricaturally caddish young man we met in the previous act. Both he and Barbara, whose meeting with Isabelle follows Robert's, begin to take on the complex and contradictory characteristics of life. Barbara even treats Isabelle with sympathy, trying to shield her from some of the unpleasant facts the others are so eagerly forcing her to accept.

Georges interrupts Isabelle's meeting the members of his family when he returns from Paris. His scene alone with Isabelle provides the dramatic focus of the act. This is one of the most poetic, tender, and sad love scenes Anouilh has ever written. Georges confesses that he lied to Isabelle because he had nothing good or decent to offer her. Since he was unworthy of her, he remade himself as he wished to be, as he hoped he would have been. To offer her something pure, something decent like herself, he invented his "life." But Georges no longer has the strength to resist the imperatives of the real world. This scene with Isabelle is his leave-taking, his break with his dream of purity. They are to have only these five minutes together in which to compress their whole life:

> Let's be happy! How demanding we always are. We start by wanting nothing less than a lifetime of happiness; then we learn that a couple of stolen years are already a rare thing. Then we learn to content ourselves with an evening. And finally, when you suddenly have no more than five minutes, you find that it is still an infinite oasis. Five minutes of happiness!

Robert and Barbara interrupt this moment of extreme tenderness. Then, as Georges prepares to return to Paris, the other characters, and indeed, the audience, are startled to discover that he is wounded and bleeding. Georges, we learn, had returned to Senlis from a confrontation with Henriette. In their quarrel she shot him with her pearl-handled revolver, and when they subsequently struggled for the gun, she fell and struck her head. Georges assumes that she was killed.

After the revelation of these melodramatic events there is once again a return to comedy. The *maître d'hôtel* recites his usual hymn in praise of his employers, and as in so many farces, the curtain comes down with a character's raising his arms to heaven, declaring, "Ah, what an evening!" Thus, in the space of a few minutes Anouilh has changed the tone three times—from the lyrical, to the melodramatic, to the farcical. A remarkable and daring feat!

In the fourth and final act, which takes place immediately after the events of Act III in the same salon, we become aware that Anouilh's prime attention is not on the details of melodramatic plotting. To be sure, he does not ignore these details: we learn that Georges's wound is superficial and that Henriette is not dead and is more in love with Georges than ever. But Anouilh is far more interested in developing and shading the complex motivations of his characters. In an important scene between Barbara and Isabelle, we learn, for example, that Barbara is very deeply in love with Georges but is also aware that the Georges she loves is not the same as the man Isabelle loves. Barbara is attracted to the sad, insecure, and somewhat brutal Georges she has known. She accepts him with all his faults, as he is, not as he wants to be. And because she loves him, she will not try to get him back.

There is a remarkable farewell scene between Georges and Barbara, which is a counterpart of the love scene between Georges and Isabelle in Act III. It is, for the world of reality, what the poetic "five minutes of happiness" were for the world of the imagination. Both Georges and Barbara show a degree of emotion, of generosity, of tenderness that modifies quite substantially the harshness presented earlier in the play. Barbara masks her feelings, for if Georges is to be free he must not see her torment. She must remain in the world Georges has been trying to reject. Georges is determined to flee this world, to divorce Henriette, and to escape with Isabelle to the Pyrenees and raise bees.

After this scene of great emotion and tension, Anouilh modulates the tone of the final moments of the play, which provide a striking coda. This shift is accomplished through various theatrical devices that alter mood, theme, and even plot. Indeed, the very vocabulary of the characters is full of theatrical expressions. Thus, when Barbara and Robert wonder how they are to take their leave of Georges, Anouilh solves the problem by calling attention to it. Robert asks the two actors who have returned to the stage how they should leave, and the two professionals give a brief history of famous exits—as performed by Sylvain, Mounet-Sully, Sarah Bernhardt. All the while, Robert and Barbara are inching upstage to the door, until they disappear "as if through a trap door." The actors disapprove: "No one ever made an exit like that." They may be critical, but this deliberately unreal stage departure is just what is necessary, for it allows the play to return to the realm of illusion, of fantasy, of perfection. With the "tranquil cruelty of happy people," Isabelle announces that other worlds no longer exist. The *maître d'hôtel* calls them to the table, and Georges and Isabelle exit to have their "family dinner" together as the curtain falls.

Le rendez-vous de Senlis is a fascinating work. At times one has the impression that Anouilh has really written a *pièce noire* using techniques from the *pièces roses*. Isabelle, innocent, direct, pure, clearly a "rose" character, seems to have taken a wrong turn and wound up in *pièce noire*. But she is not alone in contributing to this confusion. For example, many of the very bleak details of Georges's life are presented to the audience in a highly amusing way. Moreover, in this play it is clear from the start that most of the secondary figures— the actors, the *maître d'hôtel*, the landlady—are meant to be funny. Furthermore, Anouilh's self-conscious devices in the *pièces roses*, largely stagey, contribute to a lightening and softening of the tone.

The ending, however, poses something of a special problem, for here, where it is most important, the "rose" coloration is least successful. Compared with the ending of *Le voyageur sans bagage*, the final element of fantasy in *Le rendez-vous de Senlis* is not strong enough. In *Le voyageur sans bagage* the young English lad appears only at the very end of the play, in a deliberately contrived and artificial scene; even his entrance is accompanied by appropriate music. There was little likelihood that we would be duped into believing in his reality.

In *Le rendez-vous de Senlis,* however, the happy ending is made much *too* plausible. The representative of the dream world has been on stage for half of the play, and Isabelle has become too central to the plot, too real a character, to be simply a *dea ex machina,* a dramatic convention. Furthermore, Barbara and Robert, representatives of the real world, contribute to making this happy ending possible and credible. Their motivation and solidity deny those elements of surprise and strangeness that would undermine the fantasy conclusion. In short, everything works to make the ending plausible. But we must *not* believe it. The final scene should be totally, flagrantly unreal: it is a dream; it is as much a lie as the ending of *Le voyageur sans bagage.* After so much pain and cruelty it is not conceivable that Isabelle and Georges could create a life of perfection and innocence together. Georges's sudden independence at the end of the play, his entrance into an ideal world as symbolized by his dinner with the "family," is, of course, only wish fulfillment. But no man of the nature Anouilh has described can be left happy at the final curtain, ready to inhabit his private Utopia; he is not fit for it, nor, indeed, can we believe in its existence.

Anouilh has sought to deal with his theme on several levels, by mixing comedy and melodrama, fantasy and tragedy. Thus, for example, while the opening scenes of the play are so unreal as to plunge us into the world of comedy—even, at moments, of farce—we are aware throughout the first act of something deeper and more disturbing. But for a large part of the remainder of the play the influence of melodrama is too strong. Many of the melodramatic devices seem all-too-seriously intended: they are presented rather straightforwardly and are integral parts of the plot. The result is that the necessary artistic balance is lost. This is a failure of execution, not of vision, for even at this stage of his career Anouilh is enough of a shrewd observer of human nature, enough of a clear-sighted commentator on the human condition, to realize that simple solutions, single tonalities, are not adequate in dealing with his material.

For all its shortcomings, however, *Le rendez-vous de Senlis* is important because in it Anouilh made a fruitful discovery. For the first time he uses the device of actors playing actors. The incorporation of the world of the theater into the play itself will become a major element in his future writing and one of his richest sources of irony, of comedy, and ultimately of his power. Even in this first attempt Anouilh instinctively knows how to use actor-characters as a rich source of commentary on life. They are unreal because they are not of this world. They exist apart from everyday life in order to observe and comment on it. They are portrayed both as they function in the world they seek to mirror and as they enact "on stage" the roles other people play offstage.

Although the actors have a believability and genuine comic quality that render them more than simply caricatures, more than just a dramatic convenience, Anouilh does not fully exploit their usefulness in *Le rendez-vous de Senlis*, for they hardly appear after the first act, and when they do it is only for comic effect. Nevertheless, the actors do participate in the two worlds at conflict in the play. They are real people who are very much a part of the nasty life from which Georges is trying to escape. Their art, however, enables them to "play" at roles in the ideal world, the world existing only in the imagination, only in the theater. This joining of the real and the unreal, of fantasy and reality, explains, in part, why the people of the theater, from this play on, will never be too far from Anouilh's mind. In some form—vocabulary, theme, plot, structure, or subject matter—the world of the theater will be found in almost all the works that follow.

When *Le rendez-vous de Senlis* opened in March, 1941, at the Théâtre de l'Atelier, it was considered one of the most intriguing and exciting plays of the season. Critics praised Anouilh's ability to deal with a very serious subject in a way that was only superficially gay and lighthearted. This was the second of Anouilh's works to be directed by André Barsacq, who was largely responsible for the successful balancing of its complex and often contradictory tonalities. The play was revived several times; at its most recent staging, in December, 1954, critics again found it a work of interest and quality. Jacques Lemarchand in *Le Figaro littéraire* praised Anouilh's comic invention, but even more he admired the "secret tenderness" for human beings that is a particular gift of Anouilh, a "tenderness made up of love and disgust."

In New York the play was staged Off-Broadway in February, 1961, as *Rendez-vous at Senlis*. It was a failure, running for only ten performances. Walter Kerr in the *Herald Tribune* called it an "insinuating little comedy," and Harold Taubman in the *Times* found Anouilh using his artillery to "fire fashionable puff-balls." But John McClain in the *Journal American*, although complaining that there was an "inordinate amount of talk," found the play to be inventive and "highly amusing most of the time."

Antigone and the
Nouvelles pièces noires

In the *nouvelles pièces noires* Anouilh uses myth in a manner analogous to his treatment of farce, fantasy, and naturalistic melodrama in the earlier plays. It allows him the ironic refraction, the counterpoint, the dual vision that are hallmarks of his theater. In turning to classical mythology, or to a legend such as Romeo and Juliet, Anouilh was traveling along a path that had been well traversed by French writers earlier in the century: Cocteau, Giraudoux, Gide, and Claudel. But Anouilh was not simply following a vogue. Certainly, he was well aware of the advantages of using material with which his spectators were already familiar. French audiences had become accustomed to seeing classical subjects on stage and recognizing contemporary allusions in them. For Anouilh in particular, the simultaneous unwinding of the story in the realm of myth and of reality permitted the heightened theatricality he had been cultivating; what is more, it allowed him to deal with themes and subjects that would seem out of place in melodrama or bourgeois drama. The great advantage of myth for Anouilh is that it presents values and ideals that exist only in a modified or diluted form in the real world; myth therefore can comment ironically on the limitations of reality.

Jézabel (written 1932; unperformed) belongs to this group of plays only through the allusions of the name of the title character. It would be much more appropriately placed among the *pièces noires*, for it is a strident melodrama of almost unrelieved naturalism, stylistically and thematically crude and oversimplified. The young protagonist, Marc, seeks to escape from his family by marrying a young and wealthy woman. But when his mother murders his father to obtain the money she needs to save her lover from prison, Marc resolves to stay with her. He fears that he has been too deeply corrupted by his family. At the final curtain, however, he runs out of the house. One is not sure whether this escape is toward freedom or madness.

Except for a remarkable confrontation at the end of the play between mother and son, there is little of interest in this harsh and unpleasant work. This scene in which the needs of the two prove to be totally incompatible—of the son for a tender and understanding mother; of the mother for the freedom to lead her life as she pleases—is one which has continued to haunt Anouilh and which he was indeed to rewrite several times in his later work.

In *Roméo et Jeannette* (1946), Anouilh's only adaptation of a nonclassical legend, the star-crossed lovers discover their love as suddenly and as fatally as Shakespeare's. When the young hero meets his fiancée's sister, a wild and headstrong creature, their attraction is terrifyingly complete. The play deals both with the increasing inability of the lovers to free themselves from the past and with their growing realization that the only way to preserve the purity of their love is to escape from the world. Rather than compromise and accept unsatisfying marriages with others, they drown themselves.

The legend of pure and youthful love should have served to add resonance to this bleak and somewhat overripe story, but in this instance the two versions do not seem to illuminate one another. There is no disturbing, revealing, or ironic light cast on either the world of legend or on that of the very soiled reality presented in the play. The traditional interpretation and Anouilh's are virtually identical—both emphasizing the impossibility of sustaining an intense, passionate, and all-embracing love over a period of time. Moreover, the specific allusions to the legend are minimal.

Two of Anouilh's constant themes play an important part in his version of *Médée* (1953): the burden of the past, and the refusal to accept a deceptive happiness. And the long scene between Medea and Jason analyzes once again the familiar Anouilh subject of the inevitability of love's destruction. Unfortunately, however, the classical Medea who slaughters her two children and murders Jason's bride cannot be assimilated into Anouilh's world. The passion, the savagery, the mystery that are the bases of the Greek myth remain unreconciled with the more realistic concerns of Anouilh's theater.

The most successful of the *nouvelles pièces noires*, and one of the most popular of all Anouilh's plays, is *Antigone* (1944). Here the interplay between his own vision and the world of legend is accomplished simply and directly; the two worlds constantly refer to one another—commenting on and enriching one another.

When the curtain rises, all the actors are on stage,

engaged in casual activities: chatting, playing cards, knitting. Anouilh asks for a neutral decor for the setting, and, indeed, in most productions the performers even wear contemporary evening clothes: bland and familiar. The physical look of the production, even though contemporary, should seem timeless.

One of the players, who serves as narrator-chorus, steps forward to announce that the company is going to act out for us the story of Antigone. He introduces the various participants in the drama: Antigone and Ismene, daughters of Oedipus and Jocasta; Creon, Oedipus' brother-in-law and now ruler of Thebes; Hemon, Creon's son and Antigone's fiancé; Eurydice, Creon's wife; a messenger, and three soldiers. The narrator also tells us the fate of each character. Anouilh seems to be insisting that we know what is going to happen from the very outset: Antigone, Hemon, and Eurydice will die at the end of the play, and Creon will be left in a crushing solitude to await death. Interest thus is focused not on *what* is going to happen, but on *how* it is to happen, and, if possible, on *why* it happens in this way.

The prologue also provides some of the background we need to understand the central situation. The narrator reminds us that after Oedipus' death Antigone's two brothers, who were to have ruled Thebes in alternate years, killed each other in their struggle to maintain control. As an example to the people, Creon decreed that one brother was to receive national honor, and the other was to be left unburied at the gates of the city. Creon also declared that anyone trying to bury Polynices would be put to death.

As the narrator relates this information, the stage gradually empties, and when he is finished, the main action of the play begins. The lighting changes to suggest the cold, pre-dawn hours, and Antigone enters on tiptoes, her shoes in her hand. Her nurse catches her and assumes that Antigone is sneaking back home after a meeting with a lover. But when Ismene interrupts this scene, the tone shifts from the amusing familiarity of the nurse's scolding to an impassioned discussion of what the two sisters are to do about their unburied brother. Antigone is clear as to where their duty lies; they must bury Polynices, no matter what the penalty. Ismene, however, is not quite so resolved; she can understand Creon's motivation. Antigone, however, does not wish to understand: "Understand, always understand. I don't want to understand. I'll understand when I get old, if I ever get old." When Ismene finishes, Antigone promises to listen to her arguments, to listen to the voice of reason, although her slight, sad smile tells us that it will be to no avail.

Antigone seems to become a little girl again when the nurse reenters, bringing her a breakfast of coffee and bread with butter. The play abounds in such anachronisms, which result in keeping the audience dislocated in time, through the confusion of past and present. In her brief scene with the nurse Antigone hints at some completed action and asks the nurse to take care of her dog if for some reason she were unable to do so.

These hints become even stronger when Hemon enters. Although Antigone expresses deep love for him, we are struck by the tense she uses. She speaks of the child they would have had, of the tender wife she would have been. As Hemon begins to be aware that Antigone is speaking of things that are no longer to be, she makes him promise to leave without questioning her and then tells him that she will never be able to marry him. "It's all over for Hemon," Antigone says softly, almost peacefully, as he leaves.

Ismene returns to try to convince Antigone not to attempt what is beyond her power. After all, she reminds her, Polynices is dead and was never a very good brother to them. Antigone smiles ironically and as she leaves the stage tells Ismene that it is too late; she has already done what she had to.

Creon enters next, with a soldier who explains that someone has tried to bury Polynices. Creon's attempt to keep the news from becoming generally known enlarges the focus of the problem by pointing up some of the political and social ramifications of Antigone's act. The narrator-chorus now steps in to tell us that everything is ready; the machinery, wound tight and well oiled, will unwind on its own. This is, he indicates, what is so reassuring in a tragedy: there is no possibility of any change, no chance of escape; there is no hope.

Antigone is led in by the soldiers. They had, following Creon's order, uncovered the body of Polynices, but Antigone, in broad daylight and with her bare hands, repeated her act of defiance. The soldiers leave Antigone alone with Creon, and the play now reaches the major confrontation.

Initially Creon does not fully understand the nature of his adversary. She seems barely more than a frail young girl, and he is deceived into treating her in a kindly, avuncular way. At first he underestimates her dedication and resolution, her readiness to die for her action. Suddenly, however, he realizes that she is Oedipus' daughter and that once more he is faced with the pride, the stubbornness, of the race of heroes: "In your family you are all ill at ease in dealing with what is merely human. What you seek is a private meeting with destiny, with death." Creon places himself in quite another world—the world of those who roll up their sleeves and try to do their jobs as well as possible.

They try to make the world a little less absurd. Creon, in his role as ruler of Thebes, tries to explain to Antigone why it is politically necessary to leave Polynices unburied, even though it is an action that revolts and offends him. Antigone, however, would have refused such a role; she would have said "no." But Creon, having accepted the role, must now play it out completely. Having said "yes," he must continue performing actions that go against his nature.

Here an essential distinction is being made between Antigone and Creon, between those who say "yes" and make all the necessary compromises and those who say "no" and refuse any concessions whatsoever. Antigone taunts Creon, for it is she, frail and under threat of death, who is free; it is she who is a queen. He, although ruler of the country, is forced by his role to repeat brutal and revolting actions. He is not free because he must have Antigone killed in spite of himself.

Antigone at this moment is in a much stronger position than Creon. He is on the defensive. Who then, he cries, is to rule? Who is to assume responsibility for governing? It is very nice to stand aside and say "no":

> It's very easy . . . even if you have to die. You only have to stand still and wait. But to say "yes" you have to sweat . . . and plunge your hands in up to your elbows to grab hold of life.

But Antigone will not listen; she merely repeats what she said to Ismene:

> I don't want to understand. That's all right for you, but I am here for something other than understanding. I'm here to say "no" to you and to die.

The Duchess (Marguerite Jamois) tries to convince a skeptical Gaston (Michel Vitold) of the value of rediscovering his past. A scene from the 1950 Paris revival of *Le voyageur sans bagage*.

In the 1947 Paris revival of *Antigone* the narrator introduces the characters in the opening moments of the play.
Antigone, played by Anouilh's first wife, Monelle Valentin,
is seated alone, third from the left.

The confrontation scene between Creon and Antigone in
the 1946 New York production of *Antigone*. Katharine
Cornell and Cedric Hardwick are the combatants.

Madame Alexandra (Marie Ventura) instructs Colombe (Danielle Delorme) in the ways of the theater and of life in the original Paris production of *Colombe*.

FRENCH CULTURAL SERVICES, NEW YORK

The farcical end of the second act in the London version of *The Waltz of the Toreadors*. In this production, much admired by the author, Hugh Griffiths as General Saint-Pé finds his attention divided between Ghislaine, unconscious on the sofa, and Amélie, unconscious in the arms of a distraught Gaston.

RADIO TIMES HULTON PICTURE LIBRARY, LONDON

Joan, played by Julie Harris, signs the abjuration, as Warwick, played by Christopher Plummer, watches from the distance, in the New York production of *The Lark*.

Antoine de Saint-Flour, played by Jean-Pierre Marielle, extols the beauty of life and the greatness of man to his son Toto, played by Claude Stermann, in the final scene of *Les poissons rouges*.

The arrival of the mourners at the beginning of *Cher Antoine*. Francine Berge as Estelle and Françoise Rosay as Carlotta hold the center of the stage.

Creon is not quite defeated, although his energy appears drained. He insists that Antigone know the truth of the terrible story to which she has committed herself. One senses that Creon's fatigue is brought on by his disgust at the facts he is about to relate and by his sorrow that he is going to destroy any illusions Antigone may have had about her family. He tells her of Eteocles' and Polynices' brutal treatment of Oedipus, of their insults and even their attempts to kill him and assume the throne. He also reveals that he does not even know which of the two corpses is which, and does not much care.

Antigone is crushed. All enthusiasm has been beaten out of her by Creon's terrible revelations, and she tries to leave, moving like a sleepwalker. Creon, confident of victory, tells her that she must not ask for too much, that she must accept life simply and try to be happy, for "life, after all, is perhaps nothing more than happiness." The word "happiness" seems to sting Antigone. She who had been committed to action even if it meant death cannot accept Creon's simplistic and somewhat mawkish view of life. She tells him, calmly but with great resolution, that she cannot live with the lies, the compromises, the cruelties, and the crimes that are necessary in order to be happy. This "little shred of happiness" can be purchased only at too high a price. She moves confidently to the offensive:

> I want everything, immediately, and I want it all, or else I refuse. I don't want to be modest and be happy with a small piece if I've been good. I want to be sure of everything today, and I want it to be as beautiful as it was when I was small, or I want to die.

Antigone reminds Creon of Oedipus, and she proudly affirms her place alongside her father, among those "who pose questions to the very end. We are those who attack your hope when we encounter it, your dear hope, your filthy hope."

Creon is still rent by hesitation, and Antigone, like a Fury, provokes him to action. Although he knows she must die, the ideal of freedom and integrity she proclaims is a cruel and ironic reminder of what he himself had sought, of how he, too, had wanted to act before saying "yes." He attempts to silence her, but she will not be stilled: "Come on, Creon, a little courage." When he finally calls his guards to take her away, Antigone is profoundly relieved: "At last, Creon."

Hemon enters to try to save Antigone, and in this scene Creon pays yet again for having said "yes." He forces Hemon to look at life squarely and directly for the first time. He tries to make him aware of the solitude that is the inevitable cost of accepting responsibility. Hemon, however, rather than accepting this truth, runs off calling to Antigone for help.

In the following scene Antigone is alone with the guard. She appears a frightened young girl facing death. The dedication and strength she summoned during her confrontation with Creon have abandoned her. In her solitude she no longer knows what she is dying for. She is tormented by the memory of her love for Hemon, of her desire for a child, and she tries to dictate a letter to Hemon. Rather than letting anyone know her doubts, she has the guard write simply: "Forgive me. Without little Antigone you would all have been much more tranquil. I love you."

As Antigone is led to her death, the chorus announces: "It's all over for Antigone; now Creon's turn is coming. They're all going to have to go through it."

A messenger enters and describes Antigone's death: She is entombed, but when the stone is rolled into place Creon hears another voice in the cave; Creon orders the stone removed and finds Hemon at the side of Antigone, who has hanged herself; as Creon enters the cave, Hemon kills himself.

Creon now appears on stage, his suffering not ended, the chorus tells us, for he now learns that his wife Eurydice has killed herself, that he is now totally alone. Still, Creon raises the unanswered questions: Who is to do the job? Who is to assume the responsibility for living? The robust man described by the chorus in the opening moments of the play has become an old, enfeebled man, now waiting for death. Our final image of Creon is as he enters the palace leaning on his young page.

The chorus comes forward to indicate that all the roles have been played out. Those who had to die are dead. No matter what their ideals, they are all now stiff, useless, and rotting. At the end there remain on stage only the three soldiers for whom, the chorus reminds us, these events are without interest. The final curtain falls as the soldiers, casually and indifferently, continue their card game.

When Jean-Paul Sartre attempted to describe French theater of the 1940s, *Antigone* was one of the plays he chose as a model. Along with his own plays and those of Camus, *Antigone* represented a theater in which the basic concern was the depiction of moral and metaphysical conflicts, not the development and elucidation of character. In addition to their moral tone, these plays were austere and intense in form. They were "violent and brief, centered on one single event; there are few players and the story is compressed within a short space of time, sometimes only a few hours. . . .

A single set, a few entrances, a few exits, intense arguments among the characters who defend their individual rights with passion."[3]

Antigone is certainly a prime example of this concept of the theater. With all externals reduced to a minimum, what is left at the heart of the play is a debate. The meeting of Antigone and Creon occupies the center of the work and takes fully one-third of the playing time. This scene, a contest of ideas, of wills, is dramatic in a peculiarly French way. Giraudoux described one characteristic of French theater as the replacement of physical action by conversation, "by a lawyer's speech of which the spectators are not the passive witnesses, but the jury."[4]

The dialogue between Antigone and Creon is the ageless debate between youth and maturity, between the hero and the ordinary human, between the idealist and the pragmatist. Throughout the play Anouilh stresses Antigone's youth, for her conflict with Creon makes sense solely because of her age. Her revolt is metaphysical, not political or social; it is the response of an adolescent on the threshold of maturity to the world, which is becoming clear for the first time. Anouilh focuses his drama on precisely the moment when Antigone must define who and what she is. Here the intransigence of youth blends with the stubbornness of heroism, and Antigone refuses any concession or compromise. If it cannot be all, then it will be nothing. If she cannot retain her freedom and self-respect, then she will not live. A stern, unyielding, and unrealistic position, it is also a noble and heroic one.

Anouilh has constructed the play as a series of confrontations, of trials through which Antigone passes in order to define herself and her act of defiance. That is why the play is cast in relation to a deed that has al-

ready been committed. We do not see the stages leading to her revolt. Instead, as in neoclassic drama, the
focus of attention is on the moment when crucial
actions have to be interpreted by the central character
and by others. We watch as Antigone progressively
discovers the nature of the role she has been assigned
to play: "There is nothing to be done. Her name is
Antigone and she is going to have to play out her role
to the end."

The transformation of the young girl into the Antigone that her name insists she be is the movement by
which the individual discovers for the first time who
and what she is. Antigone, trapped in the machinery of
tragedy described by the chorus, is going to be able to
be herself. Nothing can change the course of the action,
but Antigone will have triumphed. She will have done
what she had to do; she will have become herself truly
and completely; she will have played out her role to the
end.

But, then, so will have Creon. Although in earlier
plays Anouilh sometimes loaded the conflict against the
realists, in *Antigone* he presents a dialectic incapable of
easy resolution. Here the admirable intransigence of
youth is balanced by the clear-sighted resignation of
maturity. Anouilh's attention, perhaps even his sympathy, is split between the two—between the always
fatal results of saying "no" to life's demands and the
always painful consequences of saying "yes." Anouilh
poses this dilemma vividly and hauntingly, for the final
images of both Antigone and Creon insist on their total
and irrevocable isolation. Both alternatives end in solitude. As Creon had told Hemon, "We are completely
alone. . . . The world is empty."

The structure of *Antigone* appears to set it apart
from the rest of Anouilh's theater, for there is certainly

nothing in his earlier plays to prepare us for this spare and austere presentation. And, as we shall see, nothing that follows continues along this path. But the simplicity and directness of the play are deceptive. Anouilh has, in fact, retold the myth of Antigone in what we can call his usual binary style. The narrator-chorus, the many anachronisms, the neutral decor and contemporary costumes—all are designed to make sure that the audience is both involved and detached. Classical mythology is used to comment directly on the contemporary world.

The audience Anouilh originally addressed, in Nazi-occupied Paris, must have found the Antigone-Creon debate extraordinarily timely. But the play exerts its remarkable power beyond that particular situation. Removed from the political and social context in which it was first performed, *Antigone*, like all important tragedies, still continues to disturb us profoundly. The work offers no solutions. On the contrary, it forces us to re-examine the very bases of our own lives, so that like those involved in this tragedy we discover that, because of Antigone, we too can never be quite the same.

Antigone, first produced in Paris in February, 1944, had an enormous success. The theme of the work, the discussion of freedom and responsibility, had a burning intensity and relevance to Parisian audiences. Barsacq's staging and Monelle Valentin's (Anouilh's wife) performance as Antigone also contributed to the triumph of the play. In revivals—in 1947, 1950, 1954, and 1975—the literary and theatrical qualities received more attention, and critics were able to praise these more objectively.

Katharine Cornell appeared as Antigone in New York in February, 1946, but despite her presence the play ran for only forty-four performances. Ironically, one of the prime reasons for this failure must have been the grave miscasting of Anouilh's heroine. It is not surprising that critics had difficulty believing in this Antigone, for her youth is crucial to her character. Her motivation becomes unclear, not to say unacceptable, when presented by a fifty-year-old actress. Moreover, the appeal of the play, to many critics, seemed to be too intellectual and not sufficiently emotional. The critic in the *Journal American* found Anouilh's retelling "inordinately wordy" and claimed that Antigone herself "emerges merely as an insistent bore." Walter Kerr in the *Herald Tribune* praised *Antigone* only in very modest terms, calling it a "reasonably workable play."

Antigone was revived twice Off-Broadway, but it was unsuccessful both times. Lewis Nichols in the *Times* commented that "too much of its length drifts away in unrationalized talk by characters who are not quite living human beings." And Howard Barnes in the *Herald Tribune* found the play "remote and dramatically inarticulate."

In 1967 *Antigone* was performed by the American Shakespeare Festival Theater at Stratford, Connecticut, with Maria Tucci as Antigone and Morris Carnovsky as Creon. The play failed once again to find critical approval. Francis Herridge's comments in the *Post* were typical; she called *Antigone* an "unsatisfying, even exasperating theater work."

Colombe and
the *Pièces brillantes*

Anouilh's four *pièces brillantes*, written between 1947 and 1954, are elegant, diamondlike comedies. They are especially notable for their glittering
language, their complex and multifaceted plotting, and
the hardness and coldness lying at their centers. These
plays also continue some of the features of earlier
Anouilh plays—but in new combinations and intensi-
ties. The artificiality and theatricality of the settings is
reminiscent of those of the *pièces roses*, but the *pièces
brillantes* have none of the softness of touch, the pastel
shadings that characterize the *pièces roses*. Despite the
dazzling surfaces of the *pièces brillantes*, their somber
and even bitter tones and themes link them as much to
the *pièces noires* as to the *pièces roses*.

L'invitation au château (1947), the earliest of the
pièces brillantes, is a romantic and artificial work with
an exceedingly complicated plot. Two couples, one
gentle and naïve, the other cool and cynical, go through
multiple misunderstandings before being properly
sorted out by the final curtain. Though the action

resembles a lighthearted charade, beneath the surface there are disturbing undercurrents. Some of the secondary characters are familiar figures in Anouilh's theater—the selfish mother, the extravagant Duchess— and all their comic qualities do not conceal the more bitter and unpleasant aspects of their personalities.

Anouilh repeatedly calls attention to the artificiality of the play through various theatrical devices. For example, the two young men, who are twins, are played by the same actor, and Anouilh toys with the audience by having their entrances and exits arranged with split-second timing. At the play's end, when all the characters are on stage, one of the twins sends a note excusing himself "for reasons that you all understand." This absence is both well motivated by the action and cleverly manipulated by Anouilh, who expects his audience to function on a double level, to be simultaneously involved with and detached from the intrigue.

In *La répétition; ou, L'amour puni* (1950) wit and brilliance are combined with a depth of emotion and thought that gives rise to a disturbing play. A wealthy young count plans to stage Marivaux's *La double inconstance* with his wife and friends. Lucille, a young governess, is also to take part, but the growing love between her and the count elicits the wrath of the others, who cannot tolerate the existence of this pure love. Their emissary, Héro, attempts to disillusion Lucille and to seduce her. Her seduction, the count's flight from this world, and Héro's symbolic suicide by provoking a duel, are enacted against the stylish background of Marivaux's comedy. The characters in Anouilh's drama and those in Marivaux's overlap disconcertingly. Both plays deal with the theme of incompatibility, of the existence of two "races" that cannot be united. And Anouilh creates a marvelously rich refraction in which the "real" world of the Count and Lucille and the "false" one of Marivaux's play mirror and comment on one another.

The structural complexity does not conceal the brutal and harsh atmosphere in which the action is played out. Indeed, the elegance of the manners and of the dress makes the cruel and savage behavior the more disturbing. The worst deeds are inspired by a combination of boredom, despair, cruelty, and perhaps even sadism. The portrait is so bleak, so harsh, so brutal, that one cannot help reacting with incredulity; a dangerously deep vein of melodrama weakens the play.

Cécile; ou, L'école des pères (1954) is a one-act divertissement in which Anouilh pays homage to Molière, Marivaux, and Musset. This amusing and stylish work has a rather simple and traditional plot: a wealthy bourgeois tries to prevent his daughter's marriage to the man she loves. Through the clever intervention of the young girl's governess, all ends happily: the two lovers are united, and the father and governess are joined as well.

Anouilh wants us to recognize the familiar world of classical French comedy, but he deliberately throws things somewhat out of focus. For example, in the stage directions, he asks for costumes of the period of Louis XV or Louis XVI, "but as false as possible." This is the key to what Anouilh is attempting here. He is offering a double vision, writing a traditional scene and at the same time calling attention to its very conventionality, insisting upon its artificiality. The audience's involvement is challenged: it cannot simply respond to the surface emotion generated by the story; it must simultaneously have a critical and intellectual response to this material. Thus, *Cécile*, as well as being

a clever tribute to Anouilh's classical mentors, also
bears his very personal stylistic and thematic imprint.

Colombe (1951), the finest of the *pièces brillantes*,
is also Anouilh's first play set entirely in the theater.
All the action takes place in a Parisian theater that is
the home of the company of Madame Alexandra, an
aging but still reigning queen of the turn-of-the-century
stage—indeed, a rival of Sarah Bernhardt, whose name
is invoked several times during the play.

When the curtain rises, we are backstage in the
dressing-room area and are introduced to Madame
Alexandra's estranged son Julien and his wife Colombe.
They are waiting for Madame Alexandra to finish re-
hearsing her newest vehicle, *The Woman and the
Serpent*. Julien, an impoverished pianist, about to
leave for military service, is seeking the protection and
aid of Madame Alexandra for Colombe and their
infant son. Julien's appearance backstage is an admission of defeat—minor defeat, but humiliating nevertheless—for Julien, we discover, is a young man with a very
rigorous conception of personal honor. Indeed, his
notions are so rigorous, so exaggerated, that he first
seems comic—rather ridiculous and insensitive. For
example, although he could have avoided military service through his mother's influence, he is so anti-
militaristic that he "didn't want to ask anything of the
French army, not even deferment."

But the information about Julien's past revealed in
the opening scene with Madame Georges, the star's
dresser, offsets some of his ridiculousness. We discover
that his childhood was marked by terrible deprivation,
both physical and emotional. Julien's father, a soldier,
was a difficult man, one whom everyone found impossible, and like a properly comic misanthrope, he fell in

love with precisely the wrong woman, Madame Alexandra. When she left him after three weeks, Julien's
father shot himself, and Julien was born because abor-
tions were too difficult to arrange while on tour. While
an infant, he was passed on to the care of others:

> The only times I was able to speak to mother were
> when she was playing a mother that evening. In
> spite of all one says about it, the theater is still
> good for something.

Julien's attitude toward his mother is understandably
less than devoted.

The entrance of Madame Alexandra—surrounded by
an entourage consisting of a hairdresser, a stage manager, a secretary, a chiropodist, and a manicurist—cuts
short this expository scene. She sweeps past them into
her dressing room, and the remainder of Act I is divided between this inner circle of Madame Alexandra's
world, her dressing room, and the outside world, symbolized by the corridor in which Julien is forced to wait.

Madame Alexandra is revealed as a true *monstre de
théâtre*. All the frenzied activity, at once comic and
terrifying, makes Julien aware of his error in having
come to her for help. But as the young couple is about
to leave, Julien's brother Armand enters. Armand is a
member of Madame Alexandra's acting company; in
personality and appearance he is all that Julien is not:
agreeable, diplomatic, handsome, and quite at home
backstage. He insists on persuading Madame Alexandra
to help Colombe and her child, and indirectly Julien.

While Armand is arranging Colombe's future with
Madame Alexandra, Julien tries to warn his wife of the
temptations she is going to face. Although she may be
dazzled by all she sees, he warns her not to be caught
up by the allure of this life. Colombe, for her part,

cannot understand how things that are pleasant and easy can be bad. While her husband is something of an ascetic and a moralist, she is an innocent hedonist. Their basic incompatibility is made clear during a somewhat ridiculous but touching scene during which Julien insists, "If you love me, Colombe, you shouldn't like any of the things you like." It becomes more and more obvious to the audience during this scene that Julien is in love with his image of an ideal wife, that he loves Colombe not for her real qualities, but for those attitudes and traits he projects onto her. Although neither is willing to admit it, the distance between them is wide and growing wider.

With Julien left symbolically outside, Colombe enters Madame Alexandra's dressing room, to be swallowed up in a scene of boisterous confusion, very funny to the audience but dazzling to the young and inexperienced Colombe. The seduction of this innocent is a very easy matter; by comparison, the serpent in Eden had a difficult time. Madame Alexandra reigns over everything with callous indifference and hauteur. She offers Colombe a role in her new play, and like some grotesque fairy godmother transforms Colombe's appearance. When Julien finally goes into the dressing room after Madame Alexandra has left, ignoring him once again, he no longer recognizes his Colombe. Colombe, however, seems to have found herself, for she keeps repeating, "It's me! It's me!" The first act curtain falls on these two, together in the darkened dressing room, each in his own world.

At the end of the first act Colombe is established as a sympathetic character, her movement toward self-realization in sharp contrast with Julien's rigid, selfish, and puritanical behavior. Her spontaneity and innocence make her initially more attractive than Julien, with his gruff and abrasive personality. In the first act we see the kind of love Colombe rejects; in the second act we learn of the alternatives the world of theater offers.

In the opening scene of Act II, set on the empty stage of Madame Alexandra's theater, Colombe is told by her mother-in-law about a kind of love that is little more than a succession of grotesque caricatures of passion. Madame Alexandra's lovers were obliged to enter lion cages, set fire to houses, or devour rats at Maxim's to express their devotion or to inspire her to new heights of feeling. She has fashioned her life in her own image of the eternal woman. And a glance at the titles of some of the plays in her repertory indicates the type of grandly sentimental characters she portrays on stage: *The Empress of Hearts, The Woman and the Serpent*, or *The Marchioness of Love*.

Colombe's *éducation sentimentale* continues through the offices of the aged leading man, the producer, and the resident poet. Each is interested, or so he claims, in assisting her; each offers her private coaching, "a thimbleful of port, and a couple of biscuits." Their vocabulary is the same, their attempts at seduction almost ritualized. Armand, too, offers his help to Colombe, but he—younger, more charming, and more subtle—has no trouble achieving what his rivals had sought. On the same bare stage on which the entire act takes place he rehearses with Colombe a romantic scene from Madame Alexandra's new play, and under the cover of their dialogue they are able to speak of their growing attraction. When, in the final moments of the act, they repeat lines from this scene, they drop the pretense of acting. Colombe at the end of Act II is on the verge of confirming all of Julien's worries in Act I about where life in the theater will lead her.

Three months have elapsed between the second and third acts. Julien is back on furlough because of a letter from Madame Alexandra's secretary, La Surette, about Colombe's infidelity. When they meet backstage at the beginning of Act III, La Surette cynically enjoys showing Julien how to play the role of cuckold. With infuriating detail and unpleasant precision he describes the doubts, the jealousies, and the self-scorn that characterize the betrayed husband.

The scene between Julien and Colombe that follows reveals just how completely these two have grown apart. It becomes painfully clear to Julien how terrible a mistake it was to have left Colombe in this "rotten world." She refuses to change her dinner plans, even though Julien has only one night's leave; the chance to meet a producer and win the role of Miss Income Tax in the new revue at the Folies Bergères is more important to her than whatever remains of her feelings for Julien. During their quarrel in her dressing room the whole company listens at the door. Although Julien is fighting to retain his world, the scene itself is played like farce. When Julien, trying to discover the identity of her lover, calls her a whore, she "faints." But the moment that La Surette says, "On stage for the first act," Colombe miraculously regains consciousness and wonders whether her hair is disarrayed. Colombe's theatrical behavior in this scene shows the extent to which she has become a part of Madame Alexandra's world. Her vocabulary and her actions reveal a coldness and a cynicism that, if they have not yet reached the heights of Madame Alexandra's monstrousness, are surprisingly close. In trying to defend herself, Colombe displays a hardness, vulgarity, and pettiness that can only be the blossoming of her real nature in the congenial atmosphere of Madame Alexandra's environment. Colombe, named for the dove, is destined to become like Madame Alexandra, a plumed *monstre sacré*, a bird of prey.

As soon as Armand enters, Julien realizes that his half-brother is his wife's lover. Julien finds it incomprehensible that Colombe's choice is a man who, for all his outward charm and grace, is weak, cowardly, and cynical: "Kiss me the way you kissed her. I want to know what it felt like. I want to understand in order not to go mad." He kisses Armand. As the third-act curtain falls, Julien pushes him away, crying out desperately, and somewhat foolishly, "I don't understand."

The fourth and final act opens with the closing moments of a performance of *The Marchioness of Love*, Madame Alexandra's current vehicle. The first three acts have shown the harshness of life backstage; this presentation of "life" before the footlights provides an ironic commentary on what we have seen before. The text itself, in alexandrine verse, is foolish, sentimental, and somewhat cynical. The young Marchioness, played by Madame Alexandra, has been discovered by her husband with her lover. The two men must put aside their anger because war has been declared and France is in danger; they must act according to the tenets of duty and honor. After they leave, the Marchioness and Clorinde (played by Colombe) go off in search of new adventure, for, as the Marchioness tells Clorinde:

> I am a woman. I am only twenty and I must
>   have my way.
> Come, let us both, till break of day
> Forget my love, in the arms of love.

The appropriateness of the play-within-the-play is clear to the audience, but what is not certain is Anouilh's tone. He provides no stage directions to indicate whether this performance is to be played seriously or mockingly. It would be easy enough, too easy perhaps, to play the scene strictly for laughs, with Madame Alexandra as a caricature of youth and passion. On the other hand, it would be more ironic were the scene in some way convincing, were Madame Alexandra somehow to give the impression of youth, enthusiasm, and insouciance. Certainly the Marchioness's dialogue is exaggerated and Madame Alexandra's acting should be broad, but these were characteristics of the turn-of-the-century theater. Even Julien, surely not her most ardent admirer, has admitted earlier that his mother has great talent in the repertory she has chosen: "On stage . . . she loses eighty years in an instant. She comes across as twenty, all flutter and modesty."

When the curtain falls on the play-within-the-play, Anouilh stresses the return to reality. The ritual of the curtain calls, in itself another performance, ends with the exhausted Madame Alexandra limping off stage on her cane, suddenly her true age. What a splendid moment this is! Anouilh here catches the nature of theatrical illusion and juxtaposes this illusion and life.

With the stage gradually cleared of people and scenery, Julien and Colombe are left alone in the shadows. Although Julien finds the courage to try to forgive Colombe, she cruelly and curtly announces that she will not change. For the first time she is able to live as she pleases, free from Julien's jealousy, irascibility, and fantasy. She is aware that he was in love with a woman who did not exist, and before she leaves for her dinner engagement she tries to make Julien see that his "sugar-candy Colombe" lived only in his mind.

Rejected by Colombe, Julien turns to Madame Alexandra in a futile request for maternal love and protection. But he is naturally defeated: "What do you mean,

'Mother'? Have you gone mad? Get away, you're mess-
ing up my hair." So much for motherhood in Anouilh's
world. Sentimental ideals, Madame Alexandra claims,
are a lot of rot and nonsense; life is a terrible process
of decay and decomposition:

> We grow old; we rot where we stand. We simmer
> our bodies on a very low light throughout our lives
> so that they will be ready for the day the worms
> get them.

Accepting the small pleasures day by day and asking
for no more than one can give make life endurable,
according to Madame Alexandra:

> We exchange little caresses in passing, a small
> greeting—you give me one, I'll give you one. You
> exchange a little pleasure, but you know full well
> what it is worth. And you each go your own way
> to lead your little antlike existences. You go on
> alone with your bundle of guts, the only thing
> which is truly your own.

Her parting words to her son pinpoint the way most
people are likely to respond to the Juliens of the world:
"If you don't want to wind up like your father, try
being a little less of a pain in the ass, my boy."

At the end of this scene with his mother, Julien,
collapsing with his head in his hands, cries, "I can't go
on." But the play does not end on this display of self-
pity. Instead, Anouilh has Julien sit down at the piano
on stage, and the final episode is a flashback in Julien's
mind to his first meeting with Colombe, two years
before the events of Act I. Colombe, a young girl who
comes to deliver flowers to Madame Alexandra, rejects
the older woman's offer of a career in the theater.
Watching her, Julien believes that life is good, that

perhaps theater people are not as ugly or evil as he had thought. Attracted by Colombe's purity and integrity, Julien is convinced that with her he has a chance for happiness. Suddenly the possibility of hope awakens in the rather sad young man. As the final curtain falls, the two young people run off together, sure of their love, sure of their happiness, sure of the future. Enthusiastically they cry out across the bare stage, "We don't have a minute to lose."

Anouilh could well have begun with this scene, but how much more effective it is, how much deeper the irony, when it is positioned at the conclusion. Ending the play with this idealistic vision of pure romance heightens the bitterness. We know that the idealistic young man will come to the brink of despair, and the innocent young woman will lose her purity. The painful truth underlining the final love scene is precisely the double vision Anouilh has asked us to supply throughout the play. Although another playwright might have used the closing lines to relieve the almost total bleakness, Anouilh taunts the audience with the specter of promise unfulfilled.

There seems no possibility of a middle ground in this play: either one accepts the world as it is, participating in its corruption, like Colombe; or one chooses uncompromising purity and is destroyed, like Julien. Man in Anouilh's plays is the victim of his own nature, not of divine malediction; there is no "infernal machine" as in Jean Cocteau's play. Julien is chiefly responsible for what befalls him. It is entirely his idea to bring Colombe into the world in which she will discover her true self. He also loses Colombe through his stubbornness and his egotism. As for Colombe, although we may initially admire her quest for identity through breaking away from a domineering and somewhat ridiculous husband, her self-discovery is no noble realization of the Socratic principle. Her nature is shown to be cruel and corrupt; she would probably have done better to imitate a virtue she lacks than to be true to herself. Her youth, beauty, and naïveté are in stark contrast to the grotesques around her, but, ironically, she is not different from them, only less fully developed.

Although Anouilh's interest in the play, and ours, is divided between the two central figures, his sympathies clearly lie with Julien. This is the first appearance in his theater of the "grouch" as hero. Julien, gruff and bearlike, is the forerunner of many of Anouilh's later protagonists. *Colombe* represents an important transition in Anouilh's theater. The appealing young woman who was so pivotal in his earlier work is matched with and ultimately supplanted by a more complex and disturbing male figure, that of the misanthrope. And Julien is indeed reminiscent of the protagonist of Molière's *Le misanthrope*, the archetypal outsider in French comedy. Both Julien and Molière's Alceste are demanding, uncompromising, and irascible young men who are considered nuisances by those around them. They are irritating because they point out the baseness of society by their refusal to compromise or adjust. Their deep-seated need for integrity and honesty sets them at odds with the rest of the world. And they are both in the ridiculous position of being in love with precisely the wrong person (or in love with any person, given their natures). Alceste and Julien illogically love those women who seem to embody the values that the corrupt world prizes and they most detest. Both plays are about incompatibility, about irreconcilable differences between a man and a woman. Both plays are devastating in their portrayal of love, and both are unsparing in their treatment of their protagonists. At the end of *Le misanthrope* Alceste threatens to flee all human contact; and Anouilh's misanthrope is left alone with his thwarted dream at the final curtain. But Anouilh's picture is a shade darker than Molière's. Anouilh's estimate of Molière as one of the blackest of all comic writers may well tell us more about Anouilh than about Molière, for this interpretation may be a projection of Anouilh's own pessimism. In *Colombe* one finds none of the confidence in man, none of the faith in reason, none of the trust in the norm that prevail in much of Molière's writing.

By the time he wrote *Colombe* Anouilh found a technique that brilliantly combines wit and urbanity with a deep pessimism. And the theater itself, which he uses to a greater or lesser degree in all the *pièces brillantes*, here becomes the central metaphor for life itself. By using this world Anouilh is able to follow Giraudoux's idea of being "real in the unreal," of telling the truth but avoiding straight realism. Although the characters in the play are nastier and more repulsive than one might find in more realistic writing, Anouilh makes their responses believable by setting the action in a milieu in which larger-than-life behavior is the norm. By exaggerating the defects of human nature, the philosopher-playwright, the moralist-playwright, is better able to reveal the veniality of a society that repeatedly undermines any attempts at honesty, purity, or happiness. Such gravely serious material is dealt with, most often, in *Colombe*, in scenes approaching either farce or high comedy. Laughter and tears are seldom separable from this point on in Anouilh's career.

Colombe opened at the Théâtre de l'Atelier in February, 1951, and was not among Anouilh's more triumphant premieres. Although such esteemed critics as Gabriel Marcel in *Les nouvelles littéraires* spoke appreciatively of Anouilh's "extraordinary theatrical gifts and his prodigious sense of the stage," the biting and scathing nature of the satire were not attractive to the general public and most reviewers. In subsequent revivals, however, both the tolerance of the audience and the focus of the production seem to have changed. In 1954 the play was successfully revived, and twenty years later it was again warmly received. Critics of the 1974 production were not so interested in the story of Julien and Colombe as they were in the grotesque world of the theater. This element of the play, Matthieu Galey in *Les nouvelles littéraires* wrote, "astounds and amazes us."

When the play was staged in New York as *Mademoiselle Colombe* in January, 1954, critics found its cynicism "repellent" and its intellectuality unviable for Broadway audiences. Even with such fine performers as Julie Harris, Eli Wallach, and Edna Best in the leading roles, the play lasted only a month. Brooks Atkinson in the *Times* found *Mademoiselle Colombe* a "tired piece of work," and Walter Kerr in the *Herald Tribune* wrote of its lack "of any genuine emotional interest." In the *World Telegram and Sun* William Hawkins observed that the play "springs from a mind that has a Jovian way of howling with laughter at ludicrous, weary, everyday habits we claim as standard human behavior."

When *Mademoiselle Colombe* was revived Off-Broadway in 1965 it failed again. Critics found the characters unbelievable and the "mixture of styles disconcerting."

La valse des toréadors
and the *Pièces grinçantes*

As their name indicates, the *pièces grinçantes*
are jarring and grating plays, stressing those irritating
and discordant elements found especially in Anouilh's
pièces noires and *nouvelles pièces noires*. Anouilh, however, has moved away from the bleakly stated pessimism
of these plays. In the *pièces grinçantes* he experiments
with two different ways of expressing his cynical and
bitter viewpoint. The first two plays, *Ardèle; ou, La
marguerite* and *La valse des toréadors*, are (some time
before Ionesco popularized the phrase) "*farces tra-
giques.*" Here Anouilh uses characters who are comic
marionettes involved in basically farcical situations.
But despite the laughter they provoke, they serve to
reveal the solitude of the individual and the absurdity
of the human condition. The special quality of these
two plays results from the juxtaposition of comic form
and serious content, from the contrast between what
is said and how it is said. In the other two *pièces
grinçantes*, *Ornifle; ou, Le courant d'air* and *Pauvre
Bitos; ou, Le dîner de têtes*, Anouilh uses a different

technique. Here his presentation is more direct. The overall tone is sharper and purer, but these two later *pièces grinçantes* are less effective. Lacking the stylistic devices that enhance *Ardèle* and *La valse des toréadors*, *Ornifle* and *Pauvre Bitos* come alarmingly close to melodrama; what should be disconcerting or irritating turns unpleasantly shrill and monotonous.

The title character of *Ornifle* (1955) is an aging Don Juan, a wealthy, cynical, bored, and extremely successful poet who dominates and occasionally destroys those around him. The play is made up of a series of confrontations in which Ornifle deals unscrupulously and unfeelingly with his wife, his friends, his publicity manager, his secretary, and his illegitimate son who has come to kill him. The play, primarily a character study, has just enough plot to keep the spectator's attention on Ornifle. But his death following a heart attack at the end of the play does not seem either tragic, moving, enlightening, or even necessary. In *Ornifle* the central character is made to appear so monstrous that we scarcely care about him.

Like *Ornifle*, *Pauvre Bitos* (1956) has an unusually unappealing central character. It is, nevertheless, a more successful play, for Anouilh here broadens his canvas by showing the corruption and despicableness of the world in which his protagonist lives. *Pauvre Bitos* is the bleakest and most outspoken attack on French society in Anouilh's work. The action of the play revolves around a *dîner de têtes*—a kind of costume party to which guests come with only their faces or heads in special dress. Everyone at the party has been told to represent a figure from the French Revolution. André Bitos, who comes as Robespierre, is unaware that the real purpose of the party is to humiliate him.

The play is an unsparing glimpse into a mean and ugly society, a revelation and indictment of the corruption Anouilh seems to take as an image of man in general and of the French in particular. Because of its scathing attack, it was a *succès de scandale* when first staged in Paris. But despite its strong social commentary, it is weak as theater. The parallels between Bitos and Robespierre are arbitrary and forced. In the second act dream sequence there is no great difference between them; the mirror merely reflects the same image. This lack of another dimension deprives the audience of a major source of intellectual pleasure: discovering unexpected or ironic patterns and resemblances.

The theme of *Ardèle* (1948), the first *pièce grinçante*, is that love and life are not merely incompatible but are violently opposed: "There is love, of course, and then there is life, its enemy." To illustrate this disheartening truth a cast of comic characters engages in all sorts of ridiculous activities. General Saintpé, a middle-aged retired officer, has called his family together because of an embarrassing crisis. His sister Ardèle, a hunchbacked old maid, has fallen in love with the hunchbacked tutor of the General's young son. Ardèle and her lover, wanting to keep their love from being infected by the grotesque and ridiculous amorous behavior governing the rest of the family, kill themselves amid the farcical attempts of the family to "save" them.

The play would be simply melodramatic and unbelievable if not for the combination of seriousness and farce. Moreover, the farcical characters are more than useful theatrical devices; indeed, they accurately represent the way in which Anouilh views all human activity. We are forced to acknowledge that such ludicrous behavior may not be so alien to us. A just appraisal of the play is offered by one character, who says: "Thank heaven we're so ridiculous; otherwise, this story would be just too sad."

La valse des toréadors (1952), returns to the central character of *Ardèle*, General Saint-Pé, and to his miserable unhappy marital situation. As in *Ardèle*, Anouilh has chosen to treat the General's dilemma in a tone and style that are a combination of Mack Sennett and Oscar Wilde.

The play does not begin in a purely farcical register. At the curtain's rise the General is in his study attempting to write his memoirs. From the adjoining room the voice of his bed-ridden wife, Amélie, keeps interrupting him. Her intrusions are so vitriolic, so insistent, so crude and sexual, that the laughter they arouse derives from our discomfort, irritation, and at times perhaps even fear. Amélie is a jealous monster who seeks to keep the General living in a state of guilt and dependence. She wants to possess him completely: "Why can't I get inside your head, even for a minute? I'll do it one day. I'll surprise you and I'll kill you."

When the General's secretary, Gaston, enters, followed shortly by the General's two daughters, the mood lightens considerably. The General takes particular pleasure in shocking Gaston, a virginal young foundling, with the more scandalous details of some of his military adventures. The General's two daughters, although close to twenty years old, are ridiculous, simpering overgrown children, concerned only about securing new dresses from their father.

Doctor Bonfant enters, on his way to visit Amélie. The two men, contemporaries, exchange observations about love, happiness, and aging. They agree that Amélie's illness is psychosomatic. She is an invalid because she wants to arouse feelings of pity and guilt in her husband. The General admits to the doctor that he had indeed loved Amélie early in their marriage but that her constant reproaches for having sacrificed her singing career and his own roving eye gradually put an end to all tenderness. The General now remains frustrated and somewhat disgusted with himself: "Under this carnival disguise there beats the heart of an old young man who is still waiting to give his all. But how can anyone recognize it in this costume?"

When the doctor leaves to see Amélie, the maid announces the arrival of Ghislaine de Sainte-Euverte. She is a foolish, charming, and somewhat fantastical creation—an overly romantic and self-dramatizing woman, rather too ripe for the role of flighty virgin we see her playing. She even travels, we discover, with a pearl-handled revolver as protection against unwanted attentions in railway carriages.

In their scene together we learn that she and the General first met seventeen years earlier—when she had been a young girl of about eighteen—at a ball in Saumur. They danced to the "Waltz of the Toreadors" and fell in love. In the intervening years they have met occasionally to share innocent pleasures. She has remained pure while he has remained a prisoner of his unhappy marriage. Now she has come to end this state of affairs and to force the General to leave his wife. She claims to have proof that Amélie has been unfaithful, specifically that she has been having an affair with Doctor Bonfant. As she reveals this information to the General, the doctor exits smiling from Amélie's bedroom, and the curtain falls.

The second act opens with the General's trying to provoke a duel with the doctor over the supposed infidelity of an unloved wife. The absurdity of this action is evident even to the General, and he and the doctor resume their discussion of the consequences of growing old. When the General tells the story of his meeting with Ghislaine, the doctor accuses him of living only in the past. Saint-Pé admits that he cannot accept the differences between his present self and what he was in his youth. Despite his outward changes, he feels that his heart has remained the same, that he is still the idealistic young lieutenant at the military academy: "Second in his class at Saumur. With no money, but with courage and a good reputation. Ready to give everything for France, for honor, for a woman."

When the doctor then presses him to live according to his ideal, to leave his wife for Ghislaine, the General hesitates. He is reluctant to cause pain; he cannot consciously make others suffer. Under Bonfant's prodding, however, he goes in to tell his wife he is leaving, but discovers her room empty. Amélie has left a note revealing that she can walk when she wants to, and, having overheard his plans, she has gone to kill herself. The two men rush off to stop her as Ghislaine enters. She, in turn, has overheard the General's expression of concern over Amélie's attempted suicide and decides that she, too, will kill herself. When her trusty pearl-handled revolver fails its first test, Ghislaine throws herself out the window. A moment later Gaston enters with Ghislaine in his arms; she has landed on him in the garden. Recovering from her faint, she mistakes Gaston for the General—as he was seventeen years before. Their embrace is interrupted by the arrival of the General, carrying his unconscious wife. Both women are carried off stage, and the act ends with the maid alone on stage reading Ghislaine's rather touching suicide note: "It's very sad," the maid comments, "but boy, it's one heck of a well-written letter."

In the third act the action resumes immediately after the frantic events closing Act II. The women have been given sedatives and Bonfant and Saint-Pé settle down peacefully to another of their conversations. The misogyny of both men is revealed, as they admit that their experiences have convinced them that women are nothing more than necessities and nuisances. For the General, Ghislaine, unworldly and pure, has remained the ideal, the exception. He confesses that she alone has given him the only moments he has known without fear and loneliness. Despite his appearance of strength, despite his easy successes with women, the General finds himself only an "empty shell": "There is nothing inside. I'm alone and I'm afraid." His illicit amours really only bore him now: "It is my fear of living that makes me run after women."

He has been afraid to make Ghislaine his mistress, lest their relationship, too, turn out like all the other unsatisfactory affairs in his life. He has hesitated as well because he pities the monstrous woman to whom he is married. He can, after all, remember when their love had not yet turned to cold and bitter hatred. His mood changes during the course of this conversation, and the General resolves by the end of the scene to overcome the inaction caused by his compassionate nature and to break with Amélie and think only of himself.

The doctor leaves, and the General's two daughters enter with their dressmaker. The General, who had minutes earlier been talking of pure and ideal love, starts, almost immediately, to flirt with this charming and apparently receptive woman—instinctively, unthinkingly, almost mechanically. He and the dressmaker leave to take a turn in the garden while the two daughters come to blows over their love for Gaston.

Following this broadly comic interlude Saint-Pé and Gaston have a scene alone. The General begins to play the role of wise counselor to his young secretary, casting himself as a sophisticated man of the world instructing an inexperienced youth. His is a lesson of hypocrisy, of the manipulation of social convention for personal interest. Idealism, however, is not completely absent. In an extended metaphor—the General is, after all, in the midst of writing his memoirs—he compares the ideal to a buoy toward which we all swim. If you are prudent, you move through the water using a classical stroke, following the recognized principles of swimming. If from time to time "you pee in the water," no one will scold, provided you seem to continue swimming and keep your eyes on the buoy.

But even the General cannot wholly reconcile himself to this rather cynical view. The youthful part of himself, the Lieutenant Saint-Pé to whom he continues to appeal throughout the play, is repelled: "It is ignoble to have to grow old and to understand." And what began as a lesson in the modes of accepted and approved social behavior ends with an exhortation for youth to concentrate on achieving the ideal, to seize the moment. A call from Amélie interrupts this conversation, and the General goes to her bedroom for the "last time." Ghislaine then calls from the other side of the stage and Gaston, after a brief hesitation, decides to follow the General's advice and to pursue the ideal immediately. The curtain falls as Gaston exits to comfort Ghislaine, exclaiming with the enthusiasm of youth, "How interesting life is!"

The fourth act takes place in Amélie's bedroom. Amélie heretofore had been only an offstage voice and a comic suicide; she now emerges as a monstrous and grotesque personality. Her bitterness and cruelty are especially shocking because of the sharp contrast between them and the farcical and melancholy moods that have governed the preceding acts. Amélie accuses the General of having affairs with all their maids. When he, in turn, accuses her of having an affair with Doctor Bonfant, she feigns a sort of heart seizure, and her husband is forced to forget his anger and search for her medicine. Amélie's accusations become more and more painful for the General. For example, she insists that he was never even adequate as a lover. She admits that the only reason she has tolerated him all these years is that she is his wife; accordingly, he belongs to her not only in life but even after death.

Amélie is determined to make the General pay for having turned her life into something other than what she now thinks she had truly wanted. She has an image of herself as a major Wagnerian soprano destined to have risen to great heights, but the General reminds her that she appeared only in minor roles during the Opéra's summer season, and even then was soundly booed.

When the General tells Amélie that he wants to divorce her so he can marry Ghislaine, who has waited patiently for seventeen years, his wife cannot believe his naïveté. She jumps on the bed and, dancing grotesquely, makes it clear that she has used her illness only as a means to make the General suffer. She reminds him of the ball at Saumur and the "Waltz of the Toreadors." She remembers them well, for when she had seen him dancing with Ghislaine she became so upset that she started to leave. A young officer offered to accompany her home, and Amélie, lacking her husband's remarkable patience and idealism, yielded to him three days later, thereby embarking on a series of very satisfying extramarital affairs. Again the General cannot understand why she still wants to stay with him. Her answer reveals, in its terrifying possessiveness, that Amélie's profound and vindictive hatred is almost indistinguishable from her conception of love:

> I hate you for all the hurt you caused me, but I love you, too—not tenderly, not to be in your arms at night (we never really made love, the two of us. Poor man, you know that very well)—not to talk to you (you bore me, you don't like anything that I do)—not for your rank, nor for your money (I have been offered more)—I love you because, no matter how pitiable you may be, you belong to me. You are my object, my thing, my catchall, my garbage can!

Seeking to make him dance the "Waltz of the Toreadors," she pursues her husband around the bedroom. Their movements are indeed like a nightmarish distortion of a waltz. And the curtain falls as the General and Amélie struggle, his hands clutching her throat.

The fifth and final act is set in the General's study. It is now dusk, some time after the violence of the fourth act, and the doctor enters to reassure the General that Amélie is resting comfortably. Saint-Pé learns that his attempt to strangle his wife has only made his situation worse: Amélie, accustomed to the flamboyant gestures and attitudes of the world of opera, now considers herself and the General a "couple of grand and accursed lovers." The General quite naturally feels that everything around him is beginning to crumble. Most important, his notion of still being young is nearly impossible to maintain:

> It seems that Lieutenant Saint-Pé is stretched out bleeding to death on a battlefield, wounded by some idiot who shot him in the back not even in

combat, but before the battle started. But he is going to die, nonetheless.

Ghislaine enters to tell the General that she and Gaston are in love. What is more, her days of waiting to experience love are over, for Gaston has truly profited from the General's instructions and has indeed seized the moment. The General is both outraged and despondent; he offers to fight a duel with Gaston, but, alas, the sabres are fastened too firmly to the wall. The General then insists that Gaston is not yet of age and needs the consent of his family before he can marry. As in the best farces, a priest who has been waiting to see the General enters, and, true to the conventions of this genre, the priest reveals that Gaston is in fact the General's own illegitimate son. Only Saint-Pé can permit Gaston's marriage. Realizing that his role is becoming more and more ridiculous, the General gives his consent. "Won't this comedy ever end?" he asks as his two daughters enter, drenched and simpering, having attempted suicide because of their unrequited love for Gaston.

The General and Bonfant are now left alone together. In despair the General calls on the young Lieutenant Saint-Pé: "I want to live; I want to love; I want to be able to give my heart away." But it is too late. The doctor draws his moral of the story: "You must not understand your enemy, or your wife. You must not understand anyone at all, or it will kill you."

Finally by himself, with the voice of Amélie calling from the other room, the General quietly gives the order of execution: "Lieutenant Saint-Pé, second in his class at Saumur, ready, aim, fire!" And before our eyes the General becomes an old man, irrevocably fixed in a world in which he is alone and afraid. As the stage

darkens, a new maid enters, and the curtain falls as
the General leads her out into the garden with his
arm around her waist: "It's not that it means anything
very much," he says, "but still one feels a little less
alone in the dark." This conclusion confirms the doctor's prediction, for the play ends as things do in life:
"A contrived ending, not too sad on the surface, but
one which really doesn't fool anyone."

La valse des toréadors is a play about a man growing
old and sacrificing that part of himself which, in memory at least, remained above the corruption of the
world. It is a play, then, that deals with the inevitable
loss of idealism and the experiencing of both failure
and isolation. It traces the consequences of those who
have said "yes" to life, who have made the compromises and concessions necessary to go on living. The
hero in this work, for all his shabby behavior, is aware
of his fall from grace. Painfully sensitive to how much
has been lost, he is tormented both by regret and by
the knowledge that life exacts such a price. Saint-Pé
is a very sympathetic and appealing character. Without
his idealism, without his dream of purity, he would be
merely a pitiable clown; but we have glimpsed his
soul, and our compassion is not obliterated by our
laughter.

Like the heroes of French classical plays, the General
has a confidant, Doctor Bonfant, and in their conversations the General reveals his innermost thoughts. In
these reflective scenes the clown becomes not a phi-
losopher, for that implies a vision larger than the
General's, but a man keenly aware of the nature of the
world. A frustrated idealist, the General is desperately
seeking a love that will withstand the ravages and
vicissitudes of time. He is also a disillusioned romantic

crying out, "Surely this cannot be all that there is to life. Why didn't anyone warn me?"

The comic marionette and the pathetic victim exist side by side in the General; they even function simultaneously on occasion. The role, of course, makes very heavy demands on the actor. While the other characters in the play remain one-dimensional, the General must maintain a precarious balance between sympathy and ridicule, alternating his stance sometimes within a single speech.

Anouilh expects not only his leading actor but also his audience to respond with an unusually high degree of resiliency. They must follow his sudden shifts of tone and mood in *La valse des toréadors*; the movement of the play is not linear but rhythmic, broken constantly by repeated alternations of the comic and the serious, the grotesque and the moving. Verisimilitude, strict logical progression, unity of tone are hardly of concern to Anouilh in this play. The spectator is instead encouraged to participate as if he were engaged in a mental exercise: "Theater is a game of the intellect, and the intellect, like the bee, can very well make its honey by jumping from detail to detail."[5] *La valse des toréadors* is successful because this diversity and variety contribute to the play's expression of a complex and coherent attitude toward life.

To use Anouilh's own description of *La valse des toréadors*, one can say that nothing is believable in this story and yet everything is true. The seriocomic protagonist, caught up in the most farcical situations while struggling desperately to preserve a vision of his integrity, typifies this mixture of implausibility and truth. Moreover, the unreality of the plot reflects Anouilh's view of the world. The story of *La valse des toréadors* is a caricature of reality, simplified and distorted, emphasizing certain less pleasing but nonetheless prominent truths. The grotesque and ridiculous are symbolic of the life Anouilh sees about him. Indeed, as he has said of this play, the laughter comes "even (and especially) when we should be crying."[6]

In *La valse des toréadors* there is something new, a mature note of acceptance and resignation that differentiates it from Anouilh's earlier works. Anouilh's young, demanding, all-or-nothing characters have been superseded by their middle-aged selves. And in the eternal dialogue between the idealist and the compromiser, the absolutist and the pragmatist, the weight of experience begins to fall more and more on the side of the pragmatist, of the spokesman for the older generation. The voice of the dreamer is not stilled—the youthful side of the General continues to torment and mock him, to make him realize quite acutely the extent of his fall.

Although Anouilh still shows a bleak view of the human condition, some of his responses to it have been modified. The compassion in *La valse des toréadors* counterbalances its jarring and grating qualities and gives the play its measure of humanity, density, and truth.

La valse des toréadors was first performed at the Comédie des Champs Élysées in January, 1952. It was only moderately successful with the critics and public. Reviewers were puzzled and annoyed by the combination of farce and tragedy. Writing in *Paris presse*, Max Favalelli commented: "I really do not know how to deal with this comedy, which is both interesting and disappointing, attractive and irritating." Anouilh himself was not completely satisfied with the production, and when he worked with Peter Hall on the London staging he was delighted that finally "all the laughs came exactly where I wanted them and where I had not gotten them in Paris."

The play was revived in October, 1973, with the popular comic actor Louis de Funès as the General. This time the response was universally enthusiastic. Critics who had been cool to the original production now spoke of the play in glowing terms. Jean-Jacques Gautier, the influential critic of *Le Figaro*, was ecstatic: "It is as moving as a Shakespearean tragedy, and as hilarious as a film by Chaplin."

When *Waltz of the Toreadors* was performed in New York in January, 1957, it was voted the best foreign play of the season. Richard Watts in the *Post* called it a "genuinely uproarious sex comedy, witty, ironic, sophisticated . . . filled with bitingly incisive observations of the ridiculous manoeuvres of presumably civilized mankind." In spite of many enthusiastic reviews and the presence of Ralph Richardson as the General, the play did not find vast audiences and ran for only 132 performances. The reviewer in *Variety* had indeed wondered whether the combination of hilarious comedy and sardonic wisdom could prove popular on Broadway; he felt that the play was a "bit cynical for mass popularity." His doubts seem to have been well founded. But the play was successfully revived in New York by the Circle in the Square company as part of its 1973–74 season. Eli Wallach and Anne Jackson were highly praised in the leading roles.

L'alouette and the Pièces costumées

The three *pièces costumées*—*L'alouette*, *Becket*, and *La foire d'empoigne*—are not, as the name implies, costume dramas. In these plays Anouilh uses historical material in the same way and for the same purposes he used myth and legend in the "Greek" plays: he intentionally creates a critical distance between the spectator and the play, a distancing that is, indeed, one of the bases of his theatrical method. Accordingly, it would be wrong to approach these "history" plays in terms of authenticity or accuracy. After completing *L'alouette*, Anouilh revealed that he had started to write "without an outline, without dates, without documents, using my childhood memories, with nothing but an inexplicable joy."[7] And six years later, when *Becket* was staged, he asserted even more strongly his rejection of a too-strict adherence to historical accuracy: "I didn't look in any book to find out who Henry II really was, nor even Becket. I created the king I needed, and the ambiguous Becket I needed."[8]

Becket (1959) is perhaps the most straightforward of

the *pièces costumées*, for here the historical background is used quite directly and literally; the important episodes are acted out before us. Anouilh retells
the story of the conflict between King Henry II of
England and Thomas à Becket. After the King names
Thomas Archbishop of Canterbury, the two formerly
close friends are forced by their roles to become rivals.
Becket discovers that he must follow God rather than
his King, and he becomes the enemy of the crown. The
conflict over service to the King and service to God
ends with Becket's murder by the King's followers. The
final note of the play is ironic and mocking as Henry,
responsible for Becket's death, orders the slayers to
take charge of the investigation of the murder.

The play focuses on Becket's discovery that in honor-
ing God he has found the purpose for his life. His discovery is sudden and surprising, for nothing in his past
prepared him for it. As a result of a kind of explosion of
grace in his soul, of an epiphany of his true role, of a
new awareness of duty, Becket insists on playing his part
to the end. Indeed, he uses words similar to those Antigone uses to Creon: "I'm not here to convince you. All
I have to do is say 'no' to you."

As an historical drama *Becket* presents a wide and
varied range of materials. Anouilh found it necessary to
invent many details that cater perhaps somewhat too
obviously to the popular desire for sensational incidents,
or easy and familiar explanations. Some of these details
of plotting may be initially dramatic, but often they
raise irrelevant and misleading issues that at times dis-
tract dangerously from the serious conflict that is the
essence of the play.

La foire d'empoigne (1962) is a melodramatic (the
choice of word is Anouilh's) retelling of the Hundred
Days—the period between Napoleon's return to Paris

after his escape from Elba, and his abdication in favor of Louis XVIII. Napoleon and Louis are interchangeable characters (the same actor plays both roles) so that Anouilh can demonstrate the fundamentally immoral and petty nature of those in power. The play is history as seen on the stage of the Théâtre du Châtelet —noted for its overly elaborate productions of operetta. Indeed, Anouilh wrote of the play:

> French history is, alas, Châtelet. A few aged stars using time-worn tricks, always the same, and a pick-up company of actors, badly paid, periodically slaughtered, and always letting themselves be carried away by their great men.[9]

It is surprising that this play was accepted by the Comédie Française, France's national theater; it is not surprising that it was never staged there. The harshness of its commentary, even though expressed with great wit, would surely have offended the political Establishment. Moreover, Anouilh refused to have any of his works performed in the national theater during the presidency of Charles de Gaulle—one of the "aged stars" to whom he was undoubtedly referring.

Anouilh's most experimental dramatization of history is found in the earliest of the *pièces costumées*, *L'alouette* (1953). The story of Joan of Arc is written in a disarmingly simple tone, one reinforced by Anouilh's adopting images and attitudes from popular histories. The legend is given a child's-storybook treatment: reassuring, uncomplicated, artificial. As one of the characters remarks, "Obviously, it didn't really happen like that." The simplification, exaggeration, and distortion of a child's vision provide an appropriate as well as convenient dramatic angle from which to tell this saint's life. Indeed, Joan herself narrates some of the scenes. But such an approach to events cannot deal with the more serious and agonizing side of her story, a side that at times completely transcends Joan's limited understanding. For these moments Anouilh shifts both the angle of his vision and his structural approach, and he creates a debate, a device he already used successfully in *Antigone*. In addition, Anouilh places, somewhat on the sidelines in the early scenes of the play, two critical and clear-sighted observers, Cauchon and Warwick, who are able to comment directly and pertinently on the events. They are especially effective at those moments when the naïve simplifications threaten to dominate the play.

As the play begins, the curtain rises on a neutral, unlocalized setting with some benches, a stool, a throne, and bunches of faggots. These props suggest the most important moments of Joan's story: her meeting with the Dauphin, her trial, and her execution. As the actors enter, they carry with them additional props. Their informality, the almost mechanical way in which they arrange the stage, is intended to create the impression of a group of actors returning to a theater about to repeat a play they have performed many times. But as soon as they begin to speak, we discover that they are not players, but rather characters in Joan's life reenacting her story. Everything has already happened. It is fixed and unchangeable. The legend will be replayed, following its strict and inflexible sequence.

The point at which to start the account of Joan's life is determined by Cauchon, the Bishop of Beauvais. Despite the wish of Warwick, the representative of the victorious English forces, to begin with Joan's trial and execution, Cauchon insists that they must enact her whole career. He calls Joan forth, and she recounts the time she first heard voices. She describes in familiar, simple terms, the visitation of Saint Michael. Speaking through her (Joan changes her tone of voice when repeating his words), he tells her that she must go to the aid of France and accomplish the crowning of the Dauphin at Reims.

Several times her narration is interrupted by the comments of Cauchon and Warwick, and even more strikingly by two figures who play important roles at her trial. These two men, the Promoter (prosecutor) and the Inquisitor, question Joan about the nature of her visions and about the state of her soul.

When she resumes her story, we witness a scene in which Joan, although she has resisted her voices for three years, is beaten by her father. He thinks at first that she has a lover, later that she is mad. When her mother enters to comfort her she, too, fails to understand Joan, thinking that the young girl merely wants to run off with the soldiers.

Abandoned by her parents, Joan tells the Archangel that what he is asking is impossible. But Saint Michael answers:

> God has not come to make things easier, he has come so that everything will be even more difficult. He does not ask the impossible of everyone. But of you, he does ask it. He doesn't think anything is too difficult for you.

Furthermore, she voices his warning that she must control her pride; because her mission and role are unique, she must be "sufficiently humble in God's hands to accept this mantle of pride."

In the next scene Joan seeks to follow the promptings of her voices. She has come to Vaucoulours to get a horse and an armed escort from the gruff and some-what simple nobleman, Baudricourt. This is Joan's first success, and it is presented as a comic action, full of down-to-earth and oversimplified details. Baudricourt is a rustic, slow-witted man, and Joan's victory here is a result of her common sense and peasant craftiness. She persuades Baudricourt that what she wants was his idea all along, and at the end of the scene Joan has her escort, horse, and men's clothing. She is ready to ride to Chinon to meet the Dauphin.

Warwick and Cauchon, who have been watching, now interrupt the forward momentum of the narrative. Although he found the interview with Baudricourt "somewhat coarse," Cauchon admits that his admira-tion for Joan will lead him to want to save her. Since he came to know Joan only at the time of her trial, Cauchon naturally refers to aspects of her history that have not yet been reenacted for us. For Cauchon, Joan represents the courage and tenacity of the individual—a reaffirmation of the spirit of man. Her simple faith, her struggle against the English, remind him, as well as the others who have cooperated with France's enemy, what his true role should have been. Although such cooperation with the English—Cauchon uses the word "collaboration"—was the reasonable position, honor should have "had us attempt the impossible" against the enemy. Saving Joan would salvage something of this lost honor.

Joan's story continues with the dramatization of her meeting with the Dauphin at Chinon. We first see him, his wife, his mother, and his mistress involved in comic and petty squabbling typical of all of Anouilh's domestic scenes. Through this bickering the Dauphin is revealed as a weak, cowardly, and bored young man. When he decides to receive Joan, he plans to trick her.

He dresses his page in his clothing and places himself among his courtiers. When Joan enters, looking lost and frightened, she does not fall into the trap; unhesitatingly, she goes directly to the Dauphin and kneels before him. In a private meeting with him she gradually overcomes Charles's fears through her simple lessons of faith and courage. She convinces him that only intelligent people are afraid, but they must control their fear and go on despite it. Charles, summoning all his courage in one huge effort, names Joan to command the royal army over the objections of his advisors. The scene ends as Joan and Charles kneel to thank God, with the frightened Archbishop mechanically pronouncing his blessing.

In performance the end of this scene marks the intermission, for the play is not divided into acts or numbered scenes. The second part opens with the tableau of the Archbishop's benediction and Warwick's comments on the artificiality of this reenactment: "Obviously it really didn't happen exactly like that." He then reveals some of the political reasons for Joan's success and, indeed, although she is his enemy, he even speaks of her with admiration. He calls her the lark (*l'alouette*) who sings a joyous and absurd song in the skies of France.

When the narrative of Joan's story is resumed, she has been captured at Compiègne and deserted by Charles. Her voices have been silent and she now faces her most difficult moment—her trial—totally alone. Cauchon is the first to question Joan. He is methodical, reasonable, and understanding as he tries to convince her that the Church's doubts about her mission and the genuineness of her voices are logical and defensible. But Joan responds instinctively and obstinately. She answers Cauchon, "like a stubborn willful little girl": "My right is to continue to believe and to continue to say 'no' to you." Joan's refusal, however, is not merely the result of stubbornness—although this, too, plays a role here. Her determination is, above all, a manifestation of her faith in the possibilities of man. She tells Cauchon that God's true miracles "must be those that men do all alone, with the courage and intelligence that He has given them." This belief is in direct conflict with the traditional view held by Cauchon and the other orthodox representatives of the Church. To them, "Man is nothing but sin, error, blunder, and impotence." Although Joan has seen this side of man in her experiences among the soldiers, she regards man as capable of good as well. For her, this issue is at the very core of man's nature: "God created him precisely for this contradiction."

To protect the power of the Church, the Inquisitor must crush those individuals like Joan whose strength allows them to persevere when completely alone. This "insolent race," which forever says "no," is both more dangerous and more difficult to conquer than any devil; such behavior is contagious and must be destroyed. No matter what the price, man's spirit must be broken; he must be forced to say "yes"; he must be forced to bend to the authority of the Church.

Cauchon is much more compassionate in his questioning of Joan. Even when he orders the executioner to describe the long agony of being burned at the stake, Cauchon is attempting to save her. After this, he tries an appeal to her reason, to her common sense. He is most successful with her, however, when he asks for sympathy:

> I beg you even because I know that you are tender-hearted. I am an old man. I do not expect any-

> thing much any more of this world. I have killed
> a great deal, as have we all here, in order to defend
> the Church. It is enough. I am tired. Before I die
> I don't want to kill another young girl. Help me,
> help yourself, too.

As a result of this last plea, Joan agrees to sign the
abjuration confessing to the sin of pride and to the
blasphemy of wearing men's clothing. For this sub-
mission, her life is to be spared. She will not be ex-
communicated; but, Cauchon tells her, she will have to
spend the rest of her days in prison.

As Joan is led away, Anouilh presents us with a brief
and sardonic glimpse of the King to whom she has
dedicated her life. He is surrounded and dominated
once again by his mother and mistress, who assure
Joan that "you leave everything in order in the French
court."

In the prison scene that follows, Joan's doubts torment her. Only after Warwick enters does she gradually become again aware of her real destiny. The feelings of self-doubt and defeat that brought her to sign
the abjuration slowly disappear in the course of their
discussion. Warwick, the gentleman, the soldier, the
good sportsman, has admired Joan's courage. Speaking
to her of her purity, her common sense, he tells her that
her death would have been an unnecessary suffering,
that it would have been stupid and vulgar to "want to
die come what may, to defy everyone." But this advice
clearly defines for Joan the difference between his world,
aristocratic and untroubled, and hers, coarse and difficult, perhaps, but heroic. She now understands that by
signing the abjuration she has abandoned her ideals,
has renounced her true self: "What will be left of me
when I am no longer Joan?"

To preserve the true image of herself as the Joan who agreed to shape the history of France, she repudiates her confession. With absolute assurance she tells Warwick she wants neither a lifetime in prison, nor even a pardon. Joan of Arc cannot age, cannot marry, cannot grow fat. Comfort and ease, purchased at the cost of compromise, do not interest her. Although she is addressing Warwick, her words are primarily meant for herself. When man is alone, she says, totally alone, it is then that he finds his true grandeur, for then God shows the greatest confidence in him, allowing him to discover his proper nature, completely and forever. Fervently she declares: "I assume my life, my God! I take it upon myself. I give you back Joan, like unto herself, and forever."

Preparations for Joan's execution are rapidly made. Here the real nature of Joan's success and the meaning of her life are revealed. Joan's is the victory of the human spirit, and the Inquisitor who witnesses the burning is defeated, as he has been before, by the individual who refuses to compromise the glory and strength of man, by the individual who continues to say "no" to anything that would deprive him of his dignity and stature.

The burning of Joan is interrupted by the frantic arrival of Baudricourt. He insists that they cannot end the play like this. He points out that they were supposed to tell the whole story and they have omitted the coronation of the Dauphin at Reims. In what follows, the stage is transformed for the enactment of an elegant, elaborate coronation. On this scene, which Anouilh wants to look like a full-color, double page illustration in a gift book for children, the play ends. Indeed, as Charles tells us, the real legend of Joan of

Arc is a happy one. Her life is one of glory; hers is the flight of the lark soaring through the sky.

L'alouette is one of Anouilh's most popular plays, and for good reason. The very story is one that seems invariably to fascinate and move audiences; moreover, actresses seem spurred to great performances when playing this complex saint: Sarah Bernhardt in Paul Barbier's *Jeanne d'Arc*; Sybil Thorndike in Shaw's *Saint Joan*; Ingrid Bergman in Maxwell Anderson's *Joan of Lorraine*. In addition, Anouilh uses devices that make his version of Joan's life more accessible to a large audience than that of some of his predecessors.

In some respects Anouilh here may have borrowed from his countryman Eugène Scribe, the mid-nineteenth century playwright noted for his complex plot construction and craftsmanship. In some of his historical plays Scribe delighted in showing audiences the underside of great events, the little details responsible for major consequences. Anouilh also insists on the behind-the-scenes smallness of great events in many of the details of *L'alouette*; consider, for example, Joan's scenes with Baudricourt or with the Dauphin. But nothing is ever truly simple with Anouilh. When he presents historical figures as uncomplicated people with all their faults—*especially* with all their faults—he is very careful, at the same time, to underline the artificiality of what he is presenting. Thus, throughout the first part of the play, Cauchon and Warwick stand outside of the action, providing us with a more intellectual approach to the historical facts and the important issues involved in Joan's struggle.

Anouilh's complex technique is anything but immediately accessible to the reader of the play. In the theater, however, there is no difficulty in following the playwright's very fluid presentation. One can watch a single event colored by two different points of view with no problem. And dual or split time sequences are immediately and readily understandable on stage.

The fixed story line of the legend itself increases the sense of tragic inevitability that is so essential a part of Anouilh's interpretation of Joan's history. These events are happening according to a set pattern: thus, for Joan, as we watch her life unfold, there is no escape from her fate. In Anouilh's interpretation of her story, Joan's struggle for self-determination, her desire to fulfill her destiny, to play her role to the end, places her in that special world reserved for the heroic. She is of that "insolent race" that resists the temptations of security and comfort to remain true to itself.

Joan is, obviously, Antigone's sister. But rather surprisingly, she is somewhat less believable than Antigone. Antigone's insecurity, her stubbornness, her lack of complete self-assurance even at the end of her struggle, make her more sympathetic, more credible, and more modern than Joan. Joan, by contrast, seems a conventional heroine, and her story does not arouse in us the ambiguity and doubt that linger so disturbingly after the final curtain of *Antigone*. There is no possible question about the justice of Joan's position. This is made clear in the debate between Joan and Cauchon, which is direct and uncomplicated; in a sense, the argument is loaded. Furthermore, the characterization of Cauchon does not tempt us to think that he is right. In the Creon-Antigone debate, on the other hand, there is gnawing uncertainty for us, for Creon could very well be right.

The structure of the play also serves to decrease Joan's stature. The final scene, Charles's coronation, is not germane to the real subject of the work, Joan's moral struggle. The panoply of the coronation, with its

music, color, and spectacle makes for a dazzling cele-
bratory ending. Perhaps Anouilh misgauged its impact
on audiences, for the average spectator responds eagerly
to this unashamedly sentimental conclusion. This final
curtain satisfies popular taste so thoroughly that the
spectator forgets that the real and terrifying victory of
the play is Joan's agony and death. The strikingly unreal conclusion should mock the audience's desire for
ease and happiness. But instead, the legendary, historical, and picture-book image overshadows the personal
story of the heroic human figure. Perhaps this is the
difference between an historical drama, a *pièce cos-
tumée*, and a tragedy. Historical drama mitigates the
uncompromisingly painful truths that tragedy forces
the spectator to witness. Its effect is to increase the
accessibility of the story but to reduce its intellectual
and emotional intensity.

Suzanne Flon created the role of Joan in *L'alouette*
at the Théâtre Montparnasse–Gaston Baty in October,
1953. Her radiant performance and the subject matter
itself assured the play a long run. Critics noted that the
work seemed destined for success; some even compared
it to Edmond Rostand's *Cyrano de Bergerac* in its
broad appeal. Jacques Lemarchand in *Le Figaro littéraire* was convinced that in *L'alouette* "we have the
Cyrano de Bergerac of the mid-century." Reviewers also
felt that Anouilh had quite effectively created a Joan
in the image of his earlier heroines, and that this familiarity, coupled with the ingenious style of presentation
and an optimism unusual in his theater, would assure
the popularity of *L'alouette*. Suzanne Flon appeared in
a revival of the play in November, 1966, again to a very
enthusiastic response.

The role of Joan inspired another memorable performance, for Julie Harris achieved great success when she appeared in *The Lark* on Broadway in November, 1955, in Lillian Hellman's adaptation. This play achieved the success that had so often eluded Anouilh in New York. Robert Coleman in the *Mirror* saw in the play "flashing wit, emotional impact, and the power to make you think and feel." Brooks Atkinson's review in the *Times*, however, although generally positive, did compare Anouilh's version unfavorably to that of Shaw:

> Anouilh's reasoned speculation has little of Shaw's intellectual passion. For Shaw was a political philosopher bent on condemning the errors and malice of institutions. Monsieur Anouilh's drama is more like an intellectual reverie.

The brilliant staging—settings by Jo Mielziner and music by Leonard Bernstein—also contributed to the play's success; it ran for 229 performances.

Les poissons rouges and the
Nouvelles pièces grinçantes

The themes of the *nouvelles pièces grin-çantes* are familiar. As in the earlier *pièces grinçantes*, Anouilh concentrates on those grating and irritating elements that express so well his bitter and cynical viewpoint. But the style of the *nouvelles pièces grin-çantes* reveals a confidence, a virtuosity, and an occa-sional daring unequaled in Anouilh's theater. These works—*L'hurluberlu; ou Le réactionnaire amoureux, La grotte, L'orchestre, Le boulanger, la boulangère et le petit mitron*, and *Les poissons rouges; ou Mon père, ce héros*—are the creations of a resourceful and inventive genius, surely one of the supreme technicians in con-temporary theater.

By the time these plays were written, Anouilh's audi-ences had come to expect from him a great deal of sophisticated experimentation with theatrical form. And these remarkable works of Anouilh's maturity fully satisfy these expectations. It should be kept in mind, however, that Anouilh was far from alone in making French audiences accept dramatic innovation. The *nouvelles pièces grinçantes* were first performed from 1959 to 1970, a period in which the structural and technical experiments of the theater of the absurd were particularly important and influential. Therefore, Anouilh's audiences had their theatrical education broadened by the more radical departures of Beckett, Ionesco, Genet, and others. Accordingly, when they came to the fashionable Comédie des Champs Élysées to see an Anouilh play, their experiences in other theaters enabled them to take delight in his unconventional structure. Although not strictly an absurdist dramatist, Anouilh in the *nouvelles pièces grinçantes* engages in experiments as bold as many of the absurdists.

L'hurluberlu (1959), the earliest of the *nouvelles pièces grinçantes*, displays an interest in contemporary political and social issues unusual in Anouilh's theater. The scatter-brained title character is a retired general engaged in a quixotic conspiracy to rid France of all that deprives it of glory. His efforts are doomed to failure because the world belongs to the scions of plastics manufacturers, and only the foolish try to struggle against "reason" and "progress." In *L'hurluberlu* Anouilh combines political commentary with the compassionate portrayal of a foolish idealist, but the combination does not entirely work. What seems especially lacking here is that characteristic touch of unreality which leads Anouilh's best plays to greater truthfulness and persuasiveness.

La grotte (1961) is one of Anouilh's bleakest works. Because the plot is so sordid and unpleasant, Anouilh had to find some way to make this material acceptable and believable. He borrowed the Pirandellian device of an "author" trying to deal on stage with a group of difficult characters. But this clever form cannot successfully overcome the crudeness of the story—a saga of rape, incest, and murder. Indeed, in the second act, when the characters insist on performing their roles without the author's interference, melodrama completely dominates the play. The device of the author-as-character, which offers Anouilh the means to express highly personal and illuminating views about the art of theater and of artistic creation, is sacrificed to an unpleasant and ultimately unconvincing plot.

L'orchestre (1962) is considerably more successful than *La grotte* in transforming sordid and melodramatic material through exciting theatrical technique. For the framework of this short play Anouilh returns to the world of a third-rate café orchestra, which he had used in earlier plays, but this time his musicians are seen in performance, and their individual tales of love, frustration, cruelty, and even madness are underscored by the banal and cloying music they play. The central story of the unhappy and doomed love affair between two musicians has great sentimental potential. And when other members of the orchestra contribute their anecdotes about cruelty to children and aged parents, the work seems close to approaching the mood of Anouilh's earliest plays, the *pièces noires*. But by giving his story the framework of a performance within a performance, Anouilh undercuts the melodrama and achieves a more powerful play. The orchestra becomes a disturbing and particularly unsparing image of human activity. That these characters live desperate and unhappy lives in a world of bad music, bored audiences, and indifferent companions, a world that seems to mock their private sufferings, turns a play that could have been merely maudlin into a disturbing and provocative work.

In *Le boulanger, la boulangère et le petit mitron*

(1968) Anouilh experiments, as he had in *La valse des toréadors*, with the use of farce as a means of commenting seriously on the human condition. One of the characters in the play even says that Feydeau was the only writer to have spoken truly about the life of man. Low comedy—*vaudeville*—he goes on to say, portrays man as he really is, a superbly ridiculous creature in top hat and nightgown, "one hand on his heart, the other on the maid's rear end."

The play deals with a favorite Anouilh theme—the incompatibility of a married couple. Their individual needs are so strong, so selfish, that harmony is impossible. This situation, repeatedly encountered in Anouilh's theater, is presented as a turn-of-the-century farce. But to heighten the irony, the comedy, and the seriousness, Anouilh presents the fantasies of his characters, allowing dream and reality to exist side by side. The effect is almost surrealistic. Anouilh's purpose here is to show us a reality beyond the every day, deeper and truer.

Each of the characters escapes from his discontent in the present by dreaming of another, better, and, above all, more tranquil life. But only in the dreams of the young son do we get any of the compassion that is so important a part of Anouilh's best work. Anouilh seems to have misgauged his effects here. The ferocity, cruelty, and painful lucidity of the battling couple make laughter difficult, if not impossible. We are no longer in the world of comedy, not even of grating comedy.

Les poissons rouges (1970) is the play of this group in which Anouilh best maintains the balance between the serious and comic vision, and offers a humanity and density the other *nouvelles pièces grinçantes* lack. Like the others, the structure of *Les poissons rouges* is remarkably flexible. Its nonlinear development allows Anouilh to present a series of brief glimpses into the protagonist's life, free from any time sequence. Past and present can exist simultaneously, the one calling forth the other. It is reminiscent of the stream-of-consciousness technique in the novel.

Antoine de Saint-Flour, the protagonist, is a very successful playwright. His private life, however, is a shambles, and the play dramatizes a series of conflicts in which Antoine wages battles against wife, mistress, children, and friends in a desperate struggle to retain his freedom and individuality.

At the curtain's rise we see a middle-aged man in a child's sailor hat playing on the ground. It is disconcerting to see the child-adult questioned by his grandmother: "Did you do your homework? Did you wash your hands? Who peed in the goldfish bowl?" Warning him that he will wind up on the scaffold, she slaps him across the face, and there is a sudden blackout. Almost immediately the lights come back on, and the same man, without sailor hat, is talking to his wife about the impending wedding of their pregnant daughter. Charlotte, Antoine's cold and embittered wife, attacks him for being not only an ineffectual husband and father but also an out-of-date playwright. She blames him for the fact that their fifteen-year-old daughter is in her present state. Her question, "Are you sure you have nothing to reproach yourself with?," immediately calls forth the memory of the grandmother, who suddenly reappears and asks again, "Who peed in the goldfish bowl?"

This, in turn, seems to call forth the memory of Antoine's childhood playmate and army buddy, La Surette, for after another blackout, these two appear on bicycles wearing school caps. La Surette, raised in poverty, detests Antoine for his better financial and social position. La Surette wants to make Antoine feel guilt over his advantages. Their relationship seems based, on the one hand, on La Surette's hatred for Antoine and, on the other, on Antoine's pity for La-Surette's suffering. This compassion only increases the scorn of La Surette, who asks Antoine if he ever feels ashamed for always doing the right thing.

The action now returns to the present: Charlotte and Madame Prudent, her mother, are talking over tea with two friends. As the two friends relate stories, one about her lost umbrella and the other about her dead husband, the subjects of their overlapping conversations become indistinguishable. Husbands and umbrellas are merely things to which one clings, not out of love and affection, not even out of hate and anger, but simply out of possessiveness.

When Antoine enters, the women make veiled references to the presence at a local seaside hotel of a Parisian actress, Edwiga Pataquès. After the two guests leave, Charlotte, who is aware that Edwiga is Antoine's mistress, tells him that she intends to make him die of guilt. Then she and her mother settle down to their knitting, and Antoine reads his paper. The interior monologues of the three overlap surprisingly: Antoine's mother-in-law reminisces about her married life. Charlotte thinks of taking a young lover, and Antoine thinks about Edwiga. Their reveries end in a flaring up of recriminations, resulting in Charlotte's exiting in tears.

Antoine explains to Madame Prudent that he does not understand why everything has to become serious all the time: "Why does it have to be played as a drama? All things considered, love, politics, men, everything is really rather ridiculous and funny." But

Madame Prudent cannot follow this argument and tells him that he is responsible for all that has happened to the family. Confusing past and present accusations, Antoine shouts: "I know, I peed in the goldfish bowl, and I will continue to pee in the goldfish bowl every time it seems to me that peeing in the goldfish bowl is a profound manifestation of my identity." The goldfish, he declares, are the goldfish of human freedom. And to prove his freedom, he decides to go off and visit Edwiga. He discovers, however, that his bicycle has two flat tires, and he therefore enters the house to console Charlotte.

The first act ends with Antoine's young son, Toto, coming before the curtain to recite, very falteringly, "Après la bataille," a poem by Victor Hugo whose opening words, "Mon père, ce héros," provide Anouilh's subtitle for the play. Toto barely gets through the first half-dozen lines when he comes to a full stop. After an agonized hesitation he skips directly to the last line before scurrying off the stage.

When the curtain rises on the second act, Antoine and La Surette are again on their bicycles, but this time dressed in World War II army uniforms. The two young soldiers are fleeing from the Germans after the defeat of their unit. Even the danger of their situation cannot still La Surette's violent hatred and jealousy. Antoine's admiration for the heroism of his comrades who volunteered to stay behind, his desire to keep a copy of Shakespeare in his pack, his ability to act calmly and efficiently, are all unpardonable affronts to the self-pitying La Surette. The blundering and accusing La Surette blames others for his shortcomings and tries to make others feel guilty so that he will not have to admit his own failures:

> There are times when I wish I were a Negro or
> a hunchback in order to make you feel more
> ashamed. Or maybe even a woman, so I could make
> my husband suffer because of my poor little tor-
> tured soul.

The only respite from the monotonous, if amusing, antagonism of La Surette comes at the end of the act. In this scene, which was unfortunately cut in performance, the two soldiers are sharing a bed in a small inn and in a dream Antoine relives a moment of his childhood. His mother has come to say goodnight to her young son as she goes off, all feathers and stylish finery, for an evening at the Opéra. She tells Antoine, who tries to hide his disapproval, that she finds her husband's illness very depressing, and that she has a right to live. Without patience or tenderness or understanding, she defiantly proclaims her freedom, and she rejects any accusation of guilt or shame. Her vision of the nature of life is stern and cynical: in the pursuit of pleasure either you make others suffer or they will "devour you raw."

The figure of Antoine's grandmother reappears, asking, "Are you sure you have nothing to reproach yourself with?," and Antoine's weary sigh coincides with the slow fading of the lights indicating the end of the second act.

Act III takes place in Edwiga's hotel room. Antoine has been called there because Edwiga has made another suicide attempt. In a long discussion with the doctor who has been called to treat her, Antoine displays a rather reactionary view of contemporary society. He feels that man's strength and independence are being destroyed:

> Can't they leave man alone, damn it, and let him try to get along all alone? He is becoming weak because he is insured for everything. He is losing his strength, which was immense. He was one of the most fearsome animals of all creation.

For most of this scene the doctor quite calmly and reasonably defends the values of contemporary life. But when Antoine speaks of the twisted spirits who are emasculating modern man, the doctor changes roles and becomes a projection of Antoine's fantasy. The doctor, a hunchback, reacts violently to the word "twisted." As a hunchback he finds Antoine's very existence, his physical presence, an affront. The doctor looks upon Antoine as a premeditated humiliation, and warns him that he and his fellow hunchbacks are organized and that the International Association of Hunchbacks is fast becoming one of the more powerful forces in the world.

With Edwiga's awakening, although the details change, the attempts to make Antoine feel guilty continue. She taunts him because he has not experienced the unpleasant life she has been forced to lead: this young actress is embittered by having had to sleep her way to success. Although she first appears a comic figure—talking about her fortune-teller mother and dishonest croupier father—she gradually becomes a more serious and threatening character. She uses suicide threats to punish Antoine for not having her problems. And he, out of tenderness and compassion, is not able to free himself from this emotional blackmail. He briefly declares his independence, telling her that each person is responsible for his own existence. But when he leaves, he returns almost immediately. Compassion has once again prevented his flight.

In a desperate gesture, both amusing and disturbing,

Antoine tries to imitate a hunchback. He is convinced that unless he, too, is deformed, society will not leave him alone. This scene—with Edwiga standing on the bed in fright and Antoine limping around the room—is farcical, grotesque, yet moving. When the family maid comes to tell him that La Surette is hiding in the garage and also threatening suicide, Antoine's frustration mounts. He leaves, crying, "Two humps, I need two humps, like a dromedary. I'll never make it with just one."

After the ensuing blackout, Toto once again appears before the curtain to try to recite the Hugo poem. He makes a little more progress than the first time, but still cannot complete the poem. He is whisked off stage to save him further embarrassment.

In the next scene, in Antoine's garage, La Surette claims he is being pursued by members of the Resistance, who want to punish him for collaborating and for engaging in black-market activities. The audience is confused: we thought at first that we were still in the present; we soon discover, however, that the time is now 1944. To heighten the theatricality, Anouilh deliberately encourages this confusion. As Antoine says: "Let's not try to understand. We'll clear this up later. It must be vaguely my fault, like everything else."

If Antoine will not lend him money to escape, La Surette insists that his death will be on Antoine's conscience. Even though Antoine knows that La Surette has denounced him to the German authorities during the Nazi Occupation, Antoine agrees to give him the amount required. When La Surette tries to get even more, Antoine refuses and leaves. The act ends with La Surette hurling additional insults at his benefactor.

The fourth and final act opens with Antoine and Charlotte in bed. We gradually realize that this is a

fantasy scene, perhaps a dream—more likely a night-
mare. From the initially optimistic and tender newly-
weds, the couple rapidly changes into the irritated
parents whose sleep and lives are interrupted by the
intrusion of a child. The course of their married life
is compressed into a few minutes of stage time. This
compression is both amusing, for Antoine has great
difficulty in believing that life is passing by so quickly,
and frightening, for it shows how rapidly and irrevocably men's dreams of happiness are lost. The enthusiasm of youth here turns with alarming speed into
rivalry and friction as the husband and wife literally
toss the child back and forth between them in jealousy
and rage.

A bell rings, and when Charlotte and Antoine
awaken, it is the morning of their daughter's wedding.
We now meet Camomille, who grew up as a pawn, a
hostage constantly being asked to choose between
warring parties. Although only fifteen, she is a cynical
and unhappy young woman who is marrying a man
she does not love, quite simply to get away from her
home and family. Her scene with Antoine as they prepare for the wedding is particularly trying on him,
because he cannot easily defend himself from her
accusations of his being an indifferent father. He tries
to hide his sense of shame with rhetoric:

> You're going to tell me, you too, that this is my
> fault. . . . Then everything is my fault, and always
> has been. The Treaty of Versailles, I was one of
> the negotiators. Munich, I should have thought
> about it a little more carefully. It was I who made
> Grouchy late at Waterloo. And Genesis, do you
> remember me when I used to have a beard? That
> was me also. The whole human condition, I really
> should have arranged it quite differently.

Camomille is a strong opponent. She refuses to let him get away with such devices. She asks him if he just made up that outburst: "Put it in your next play, it will certainly get a good laugh." She, unlike the others, is able to make him acknowledge his failure. Antoine, the child of unloving parents, has grown up to become an absent parent himself. And Antoine's appeal to the "human condition," although scorned by Camomille, seems to be a serious expression of his awareness that the abandonment of children is inevitable. Just as man's nature makes marriage impossible, his nature makes parenthood equally impossible.

Antoine is called off stage by the maid who announces once more that La Surette has turned up. This time he is threatening to embarrass Antoine and spoil the elegant wedding. The following scene is a mixture of dream and political fantasy, set in 1944 in the headquarters of the Resistance. Antoine is being interrogated by the hunchback doctor of Act III. Antoine has been accused of taking nothing seriously, of failing as a father, of believing in the freedom of man, and of practicing a life style that the revolution of 1789 had sought to eliminate. For the hunchback, Antoine has become the embodiment of the aristocracy, whose grace and ease are infuriating. This race is to be exterminated so that a new race, a race of hunchbacks, can flourish. La Surette turns up as a valued member of this movement, and he threatens Antoine with death. His hatred erupts beyond control, and, infuriated by Antoine's generosity and pity, he announces that he had slept with Antoine's mother. With great difficulty Antoine controls his anger and moves toward the window to escape. La Surette opens fire with a machine gun. As Antoine starts to fall, he suddenly realizes that all this is not possible: he did not die in 1944, and the scene ends in a blackout.

When the lights come up again, we are back in the present. Toto and Antoine are heading for the local Bastille Day celebration with their bicycles. In this final scene Antoine discovers that Toto may well follow in his father's footsteps. Toto, it seems, has proven his independence by urinating on the dress of one of the guests at the tea party of Act I. The discovery that his son is a kindred spirit heartens Antoine. He delivers an impassioned speech praising the achievements of man, in which he tries to make Toto understand that he, Toto, is man:

> You are the one who invented electricity, Toto, built the cathedral of Chartres, and wrote the *Pensées* of Pascal. And they can't do anything about that. Even if they try to make you feel ashamed by showing you their stumps. . . . And Molière's plays, all of Molière's plays, you wrote them too. Not to mention the plays of Shakespeare. You must never forget it, Toto.

This creed seems to indicate that Antoine retains some degree of optimism, in spite of what he has been through. In all earnestness he says to Toto, "My little man, think of all that is waiting for you." And the final curtain falls on this tender, somewhat sentimental, but undeniably positive scene.

The central theme of *Les poissons rouges* is the fierce struggle of man to retain his freedom and individuality while everything around him is conspiring to break his spirit. The play is concerned with the nature of responsibility to oneself and to others; it deals with solitude, frustration, and, in a somewhat mocking but nonetheless moving way, heroism. Victory here, as elsewhere in Anouilh's theater, is personal—it is the maintaining of self-identity against all the pressures of family, friends, and society. The play reveals the terrible, unchanging nature of this struggle, the loneliness of the well-intentioned individual constantly forced to repeat his mistakes. But it is also an optimistic play, ultimately displaying a faith in man's ability to withstand these terrible attacks and finally to sustain honor and dignity.

One should not be too uplifted, however, by the touching ending. Toto's life in all probability will parallel that of his father's—a series of desperate battles to remain free. And Antoine's struggles are certainly not over. He has found, nevertheless, at least minor proof that he is not alone, and Toto is given indication at the start of his career that others have been through this before him. Nothing will change for Antoine because that would involve changing the nature of men, of women, of society, of the world. But something very solid and reassuring has been articulated about the existence of heroism, and about the endurance of man's integrity and honor.

Throughout *Les poissons rouges* characters criticize Antoine's attitudes, which appear irritatingly facile and insensitive. But they are not aware that Antoine, like Anouilh, *consciously* attempts to substitute witty and clever remarks in most situations for the painful reality that is better hidden. Antoine de Saint-Flour uses the same shielding devices as Anouilh to prevent harsh and unpleasant truth from asserting itself too cruelly and irrevocably:

> In the theater, paradoxically, as soon as you leave the realm of comedy, it is complete chaos. That is why, once every twelve lines I put in a play on

words worthy of a locker room attendant, or I have someone pee on stage, or anything at all . . . so that the approaching truth is never uttered. One must never tell the truth. The truth is the real source of disorder.

Critics who consider such an approach a grave deficiency, a lack of intellect and high seriousness, do not recognize that Antoine's and Anouilh's work deals with despair and anguish while avoiding pontification and metaphysics. As with the best comic writers, the most agonizing situations and the most profound ideas are expressed through humor. The function of comedy for Anouilh is to treat those aspects of life that are too painful to be dealt with in any other way. We laugh throughout *Les poissons rouges* in order not to cry.

Les poissons rouges was staged at the Théâtre de l'Œuvre in January, 1970, while *Cher Antoine* (discussed in the next chapter) was still being performed elsewhere in Paris. This made 1969–70 the season of Jean Anouilh. Two important works, both critical and popular successes, were proof of Anouilh's great creativity and durability. Reviewers of *Les poissons rouges* universally encouraged their readers to see the play. They found in it a more bitter and more grating edge than in *Cher Antoine*, but its comic qualities were, as Jean-Jacques Gautier in *Le Figaro* wrote, capable of "delighting the most ill-disposed critic and the most demanding spectator." In addition, its theatrical inventiveness and the brilliant performances of Jean-Pierre Marielle as Antoine and Jacques Marin as La Surette made *Les poissons rouges* an event of major importance.

The play has not yet been staged in America.

Cher Antoine and
the Pièces baroques

The adjective "baroque," suggesting a highly elaborate and complicated style, perfectly describes the newest collection of Anouilh plays. Baroque art, which developed in Europe after the Renaissance, is highly ornamented and embellished, scorning the simple for the complex, rejecting the straight line for the sweeping curve. Delighting in *trompe l'œil* effects, in the creation of illusion, it also enjoys destroying the illusion it creates. In literature, especially in the drama, the baroque period was characterized by theatrical illusion. The play-within-a-play was a popular device, and dramatists freely combined realistic and fantastic elements to achieve a sense of the unexpected and to express their restless and inventive energy.

Anouilh's *pièces baroques—Cher Antoine; ou, L'amour raté, Ne réveillez pas madame, Le directeur de l'Opéra*—extend his metaphor of the theatrical performance as an image of the real world. In fact, all these plays involve actors, actresses, performers, and playwrights. As Anouilh himself has said, "Theater is life as it really is."[10]

The protagonist of *Ne réveillez pas Madame* (1970), Julien Paluche, is a successful actor-director who is quite miserably unsuccessful in his private life, a typical combination for an Anouilh hero. A loving but in-effectual and neglectful father, a demanding but per-haps selfish husband, and a well-intentioned but puri-tanical pain-in-the-neck to his friends and co-workers, Julien is something of a misfit, unable to accept the many compromises others seem to make with such ease. Like his namesake in *Colombe*, this Julien, too, ends up totally alone on a bare stage.

In *Ne réveillez pas Madame* Anouilh seems deter-mined to strip his writing of all trappings—of plot, of situation, and of setting. The play is presented on the bare stage the director Jacques Copeau had demanded in his attempt to purify and revivify the French theater. Sets or parts of a setting are flown in on occasion, but each time the process discourages the suspension of dis-belief that conventional scenery encourages. Anouilh, reducing theater to its essential elements, demands the kind of intellectual awareness and response from his audience that comes from watching the very act of theatrical creation.

Of the various works that the actors in Julien's troupe rehearse during the play, the most important is the final one, in which Julien attempts to realize his long-standing ambition to direct *Hamlet*. What we watch is a rehearsal of the closet scene, and indeed, the confrontation between Gertrude and Hamlet is bril-liantly used by Anouilh. Their quarrel mirrors that be-tween Julien and his own mother, a vain, flirtatious actress who had neglected her son for her career. The antagonism between mother and son has been a key subject throughout Anouilh's career, but here, with Shakespeare's help, it is stated with a depth of under-standing and compassion rather new in his treatment of this material. The adult Julien realizes that the roles of woman and mother were not compatible in the case of his own mother. This understanding, however, does not alleviate his pain. Julien's "weakness," found in many other Anouilh heroes, is that he understands too much.

In the next *pièce baroque* Anouilh seems to repeat material he has treated better elsewhere. *Le directeur de l'Opéra* (1972) takes place in an opera house in Italy. Antonio di San-Floura seeks in the theater something of the stability and ideal order absent in the world outside. To elude the excessive demands of his family, he now lives backstage in his office at the theater. His attempt to escape is unsuccessful, for during the course of the play he must deal with the unhappy love affairs and attempted suicide of his daughter, the financial demands of his estranged wife, and the misdeeds of his spoiled, ne'er-do-well son, Toto. Apart from a moving scene between Antonio and Toto, and another between Antonio and his accountant, much of the material is familiar, perhaps overly familiar. Compared with his French namesakes—the two Antoines in *Les poissons rouges* and *Cher Antoine*—or even with Julien Paluche in *Ne réveillez pas madame*, Antonio lacks complexity and depth.

Written and staged before *Les poissons rouges*, *Cher Antoine* (1969) is, in fact, the first of Anouilh's plays to use a playwright as central character and one of Anouilh's most successful "theatrical" plays. In *Cher Antoine* Anouilh manipulates action and time se-quences with remarkable skill. Indeed, it is, from every

point of view—technically, emotionally, and intellectu-
ally—one of the major achievements of Anouilh's
career.

The play is set in a baroque chateau in Bavaria in
which the Antoine of the title, an extremely successful
turn-of-the-century dramatist, spent the last years of
his life. At the rise of the curtain Antoine's estranged
second wife, Estelle, a young woman dressed in mourn-
ing, enters with Marcellin, Antoine's friend and doctor.
Through their conversation we learn that Antoine had
left his wife for a younger woman and had moved to
his chateau. When this young woman had left him,
Antoine remained in Bavaria alone. Antoine was killed
when the rifle he was cleaning went off—a probable
suicide, although the question is not resolved during
the play.

Next Valérie, one of Antoine's earlier mistresses,
enters, discreetly dressed in half-mourning, accompanied by her young daughter, Anémone. Estelle and
Valérie have made a brittle peace, but their composure
is strained when more of the guests arrive. Among these
are Carlotta, Antoine's first wife and a reigning queen
of the Parisian stage; Cravatar, a theater critic and
boyhood friend of Antoine's; Piedelievre, Antoine's
college classmate and now a pontificating academic.
Antoine has arranged for his family and friends to
gather for the reading of his will. A German notary,
acting as Antoine's agent, informs them that there are
three more people expected: Gabrielle, another friend
from Antoine's college days; her son Alexandre; and
finally Maria, Antoine's last mistress, of whom Estelle
has spoken.

When Estelle now expresses her outrage at the
prospect of meeting Maria, Carlotta reminds Antoine's
widow of the need to maintain self-control. Carlotta

herself had done this when Antoine left her. Indeed, she reminds them that on the night Estelle and Antoine were married, Carlotta gave a brilliant performance in front of an audience expecting her sorrow to destroy her. Carlotta is proud to have transformed her personal life, her private tragedy, into art. In these opening moments of the play Carlotta is seen as an indomitable and indestructible *monstre de théâtre*.

As they wait for the others to arrive, the tension among the assembled guests causes Valérie to observe that they seem to be acting in one of Antoine's own plays; even the news of an avalanche threatening to block all roads from the chateau is the kind of device Antoine used. These comments pinpoint the major concern of this opening scene—the definition not only of Antoine but also of his conception of the theater. For example, Antoine's future biographer,• Piedelievre, wonders why so many gimmicks were used in the plays. Valérie remarks that Antoine had always despised what appeared too serious or too labored. Antoine, according to her, had felt that literature was nothing more than a "momentary diversion."

With the arrival of the remaining guests, a dull and ominous sound off stage announces the rush of the avalanche. Cravatar, always the critic, calls it "bad taste" and "awful theater," but Carlotta, with her differing conception of drama, finds it "admirable! Pure Sardou!" The scene ends in a sudden blackout with everyone at the windows peering into the darkness.

When the lights return, the characters are listening to the last few lines of Antoine's will. The notary finishes reading and discloses that Antoine had recorded a message for each of those present shortly before his death. A large, trumpet-shaped phonograph is wound up, but the moment of tension is comically destroyed as the wrong cylinder is played. Instead of hearing Antoine, we listen to a raucous music-hall song. The error is corrected, and then Antoine's somewhat off-hand but serious voice is heard thanking each one for having come so far. After describing the growing sense of failure and solitude during the time he was alone, Antoine confesses that he never gave anything of himself to the "characters in my life." In his final words Antoine says: "It is a terrible thing to be alone, for as someone once said, you're in bad company."

After this, a long silence follows before the guests, deeply moved, resume their activity. Carlotta, the realist, is the first to insist that life must go on, and even though funerals are very sad the living must eat. She leads all but Cravatar and Estelle to the dining room. Through Estelle's conversation with Cravatar we learn that her coldness and unpleasantness are a consequence of Antoine's domination and abandonment of her. The happiness of the first years of married life were gradually undermined partly by boredom, but to an even greater degree by Estelle's feeling threatened by Antoine and by her fear of losing her identity.

When Cravatar and Estelle join the others in the dining room, Valérie's daughter, Anémone, who has been sent to find them, is left alone. She replays that part of Antoine's recording addressed to her. A very young and romantic woman, deeply in love with Antoine, she is now, because of his death, determined to leave for Africa and work with Dr. Schweitzer. Alexandre, Gabrielle's (and, we soon learn, Antoine's) son enters to escort her to table. They look at each other, perhaps a bit too long, smile, and exit to join the others as the curtain falls.

The second act takes place in the same room, but late in the afternoon, with the snow still falling.

Gabrielle, busy with her knitting, is reminiscing with Piedelievre, for they had known each other years before when he and Antoine were students. She was Antoine's mistress then, and when he left her for Carlotta, she married and succeeded in making a modest life for herself, free, she is pleased to say, from the scourge of love. For her, "love is a frightful accident, and you should consider yourself lucky if you get out of it safe and sound." When Carlotta enters, Gabrielle is amazed to see in this old woman the reason for all her youthful torment. The two discuss their love for Antoine and their reactions to his leaving them. A bond of sympathy between them develops as they discuss their rheumatic pains, and Gabrielle goes off to find some of her special medicine for Carlotta.

Carlotta now joins in the discussion of Antoine's active love life, adopting, as we might expect, a pragmatic attitude toward romance, passion, and marriage. For Marcellin, Antoine's behavior was a result of his profound desire not to be alone. As evidence he points out that when Antoine left Estelle, he had retired from the world to be taken care of by Frida, the elderly woman who had been his childhood nurse.

Marcellin voices the question bothering most of the gathering: Why did Antoine suddenly abandon his family and career, fleeing Paris to live in isolation? The last time they were all together was at Antoine's fiftieth birthday party, which was on the eve of Antoine's flight. As Marcellin talks, the lighting softens, the rhythm of the actors slows, and the setting is modified so that only the furniture and the characters are clearly seen. The action has now moved back three years to that party, and we meet Antoine himself for the first time.

Antoine is clearly deeply upset at having turned fifty. This prospect has given him the idea for a new play. A man dies, not having had a very good life, having failed to give of himself, and having failed to receive very much from other people. Love and friendship have both passed him by. The day of his burial all the characters in his life come together and they sum up his life and their own. "That's all," he says, "but it will be rather comic." Carlotta finds it a terrible idea for a play because it is totally without action. Antoine assures her, however, that the play could have some amusing moments "as well as theatrical inventions—the gratuitous kind that I like so much." The play, he says, would be called *Cher Antoine; ou, L'amour raté*. Carlotta thinks that this, too, is a bad idea.

As the action of the party continues, the focus becomes somewhat muted. We can only pick up occasional phrases of the actors so that our attention is directed to Anémone and Antoine. He speaks to her tenderly, calling her the "illusion of love," the "dream one always seeks to know."

Once again the lighting changes and we are back in Bavaria, as Marcellin finishes his narration. He feels that at the party Antoine had been asking all of them "Do you love me?" and that none of them had been able to answer. The others remain silent as the curtain slowly falls.

At the opening of the third act all the characters of the previous two acts appear strangely different. Gradually we begin to understand that we are now watching actors Antoine had hired for a private performance of the play he had described at his birthday party. And, of course, as he discusses with the actors the characters they are to play we can compare his analysis of them with what we have seen and heard in the first two acts. Antoine, it appears, is trying to use the theater to get to know those "unknown people with whom one lives."

He is employing his art in an effort to give shape and form and meaning to his life:

> How comfortable one is backstage, surrounded by actors! Believe me, it is the only place where things happen. When you step outside, it is the desert and disorder. Life is decidedly unreal. First of all, it is formless. No one knows his lines and everyone always misses his entrance. One must never leave the theater. It is the only place in the world where the human adventure is perfected.

Alone with the ingénue who is to play Maria, Antoine explains that hers is the best role: "She represents love, true love." They rehearse the lines that occur when Maria and Antoine agree to separate. At first Antoine and the ingénue remain outside of their roles—they are actress and director. But they begin to deliver their words with more and more feeling, becoming Antoine and Maria. Just as the scene becomes deeply moving, however, the playwright, Antoine, punctures it with a cynical remark: "etc, etc. That was really a rather nice scene. A little too talky and literary; a little sentimental, too, perhaps."

When the full rehearsal begins, we quickly discover that what the actors are reciting is the very opening of Anouilh's *Cher Antoine*, with Antoine himself, the principal figure, providing a gloss on the various personalities and the situation.

Despite the intensity of his desire to write the text of his life, the "real text, the words one never utters," Antoine's effort is doomed to failure. "We live in cages," he reluctantly admits. "We know others only by the idea we have of them. What an incomprehensible world other people are." Having admitted that it is not possible to write the script of his life, Antoine then suggests that the actors can improvise, based on their impressions of the characters they are to play. Antoine even pretends to be dead in order to overhear their remarks. But the actors' banalities and clichés lead Antoine to despair: "We never know anything. We die without knowing. But maybe there was nothing to learn."

As the scene ends, Antoine abandons his last work. There is a blackout, and when the lights return, the notary continues his description of Antoine's abortive attempt to stage *Cher Antoine*. He explains that after this the playwright felt himself utterly alone. Although the assembled listeners cannot understand why Antoine never made any attempt to break out of his solitude, their comments reveal that each had failed Antoine in his own way. As the act ends, Carlotta, with a clear-sightedness approaching cynicism, provides a eulogy for Antoine's life: "Antoine did not give us very much, nor did we give him very much. Let's turn the page. The bookkeeping is in order."

In the fourth and final act, set on the following morning, bright sunlight fills the room as Anémone and Alexandre look from the window at the ceremony taking place at Antoine's grave site. The two young people find themselves more and more attracted to each other, and at the end of the scene they kiss. Naturally, Anémone's resolve to forget her love for Antoine by working with Dr. Schweitzer is deeply shaken.

During this scene, Frida has brought the valises on stage, so that when the ceremony is over the guests can arrange their departure. (The roads now are cleared from the avalanche.) The return to Paris and the resumption of life there becomes the subject of conversation when the others enter. Estelle allows Cravatar a degree of hope that he can call on her in Paris; Piede-lievre and Gabrielle promise to get together for a good home-cooked meal; Anémone and Alexandre arrange to continue their flirtation in Paris, both of them de-lighted at having come to the same funeral.

Estelle is left alone with the notary as the chateau is gradually boarded up: the shutters are closed, and the stage darkens. The notary comments, just about the same time that we become aware of the similarity, that this conclusion to the action is reminiscent of the end-ing of Chekhov's *The Cherry Orchard*. Antoine had once even commented to him that it was a pity that Chekhov got to use this ending before him: "I could never use it now; everyone would notice it. Or, if I did want to use it again, I'd have to find some theatrical gimmick."

The two leave the stage and the room remains dark and deserted. The noise of sealing the shutters is re-placed by the sound of cars starting up and leaving, and then there is silence once again. Suddenly we begin to hear the voices of the characters—rather ghostlike—repeating moments of the act we have just seen. It is an ironic echo of the life that Antoine had missed, the very life that scarcely misses him now. A long silence follows—as long as possible, the stage directions tell us—before the curtain falls.

Cher Antoine is a play about failure. The failure of love, *l'amour raté* the subtitle warns us, is its central theme. But along with this, and in part because of it, there are other failures: of friendship, of communica-tion, and ultimately of the ability to accept the solitude of a life without these consolations. *Cher Antoine* is a play about death, too, the death of the body and of the heart, just as it is a play about life, the choices and concessions it demands. It shows us those who are able to compromise and to continue, and those who cannot. Antoine is one who has neither the strength to endure the futility of existence nor the heroism of those who say "no."

Throughout the play various characters have accused Antoine of immaturity, a trait which he shares with other Anouilh heroes but which for him is totally crippling. He is not only unequipped for survival; he is also incapable of turning suicide into victory, of making it an act of protest, a cry of defiance. Antoine's death is instead an admission of defeat and failure. The lonely playwright dying in isolation is no Antigone.

Although Antoine spent his life in pursuit of love, each of his many affairs ended in separation, for he constantly repeated the same mistake. Women for Antoine existed primarily to fulfill his image of them. He did not act out of deliberate cruelty, but, behaving in an inconsiderate and self-centered way, he lived as though he were writing a scenario, creating the roles for the various women in his life, with the exception of the strong-willed Carlotta. Antoine was only briefly successful in shaping the lives of the other women, for eventually each of these displayed a need for an existence independent of him. Once this independence asserted itself, separation was inevitable, for Antoine insisted on writing the script alone.

Friendship, too, failed to provide any defense against the solitude he dreaded. The men in Antoine's life—Marcellin, Piedelievre, Cravatar—never understood him. For Marcellin, Antoine was simply a charming companion. Their friendship was based on self-indulgence; each tolerated the other's weaknesses, thus encouraging them. For Piedelievre, Antoine was an author to be studied; Antoine the playwright, not Antoine the man, interested him. As for Cravatar, he could never forgive the facility, the ease, with which Antoine succeeded. What began as a youthful admiration for Antoine turned into jealousy and bitterness.

In despair Antoine looked to his art for a definition and understanding of life. He had always felt there was no "salvation" off stage, but in his last effort he discovered that there was no salvation even in the theater. Writing a text for his life, like his play *Cher Antoine*, was futile because he had to provide the roles and dialogue. The limits of this despair lead to a terrifying vision of emptiness: one never can know the others in one's life, and, in all likelihood, there was nothing to know in the first place.

Even the example set by the powerful Carlotta was impossible for Antoine to imitate. Although he valued her "good sense," he could not accept life on its own terms as she does. Carlotta remains indestructible simply because she looks at life unsentimentally, unidealistically, unromantically, doing what she must to go on. She may appear monstrous, but that is only because her devastatingly blunt words are those that less courageous and less honest people dare not utter:

> Live, good God, if you can. You'll see that it isn't what you think. The gloves of virtue are all well and good, but until you've put your hands in the muck like the rest of us you've no right to sound so high and mighty. Go on and live. You'll see it's not so easy. Everyone has good intentions, but one can do little.

For Carlotta, endurance is the supreme value, and her heroism is made up not of purity and integrity but of the fact of survival.

In *Cher Antoine* Anouilh continues to explore the intellectual and theatrical possibilities of presenting an image of what is conventionally called "real life" through a milieu in which everything is artificial, distorted, and exaggerated. Moreover, the allusions that occur throughout *Cher Antoine* to the theatrical nature of the events are particularly appropriate to this story. Furthermore, these references and devices remind us not only that we are dealing with the story of people who work in the theater but also that we ourselves are sitting in a theater. Anouilh calls attention to his theatrical devices so that we are completely aware of their artificiality. An example of this is his blatant duplication of the ending of *The Cherry Orchard*. Anouilh makes Chekhov's closing scene appropriate for his play and at the same time makes sure that we know he copied it. Anouilh achieves both an emotional response from his audience and a more complicated intellectual one.

The multiplicity of responses results in still another kind of counterpoint in the play, one that is consistently comic. Anouilh repeatedly encourages and discourages an identification between the writer of the play and the writer in the play. This allows him the opportunity of answering some of the most frequent charges leveled at his art. At the same time it provides the spectator with the pleasure of watching a play, *Cher Antoine*, about a playwright who writes a play, *Cher Antoine*, about a playwright.

Anouilh employs such devices to lighten material that could be, in other hands, profoundly depressing. Characteristically, Anouilh presents an unrelievedly dark view of man; and, typically, although the message is unhappy, the vehicle is witty. The cynical outbursts of Carlotta, the sentimentally appealing moments of the young lovers, the polished and urbane disillusioned comments of Antoine himself, are all used by Anouilh

to keep us amused as we gradually approach the crushing silence of the end of this play. Anouilh's talent is
like the one Antoine sees in himself—the ability to take
us to the edge of despair by a deceptively pleasant route:
"I am the most unhappy of men, Madame, but also
the one who takes his misfortune best: I have received
from heaven the gift of turning it to laughter."

When *Cher Antoine* opened in October, 1969, at the
Comédie des Champs Élysées, it was accorded one of
the most enthusiastic receptions given to Anouilh's
recent plays. Critics voted it the best French play of
the year, and the cast led by Jacques François as
Antoine and Françoise Rosay as Carlotta assured a
great popular success. Reviewers spoke of the play's
richness, density, tenderness, and sincerity. Gilbert
Guilleminault wrote in *L'aurore*: "*Cher Antoine* is
almost an anthology of Anouilh's themes for the past
thirty-five years." Jan Mara in *Minute* found that it
was the "most 'Anouilhesque' of Anouilh's plays" and,
with Jean Dutourd in *France-Soir*, hailed it as a master-
piece, a major contribution to French drama.

Neither *Les poissons rouges* nor *Cher Antoine* has
yet been staged in New York. One wonders whether
they ever will, for the fact is that Anouilh's plays have
not been very successful in this country. American
audiences seem to have been too firmly molded by
traditions which are in direct contrast to those in which
Anouilh was formed and which he, in turn, has helped
to shape. American audiences are generally less willing
to "listen" to a play, to follow a subtle and involved
presentation of ideas. They tend to find Anouilh's work
"talky" and overly intellectual. In addition, his plays
are thought to lack sufficient emotional involvement;
an easy identification with the principal characters is

often difficult. American audiences, conditioned by the realistic-naturalistic tradition, want recognizable situations, presented directly, to which they can react with a basically emotional and not an intellectual response. When they are confronted with a theater such as Anouilh's, which is so resolutely unnaturalistic, which is involved with the interplay of ideas, a theater in which modulations of language are the prime means of revealing plot and character, they are understandably hesitant. Finally, the demands on the spectator made by the technical innovations of Anouilh's recent works in particular would no doubt make them uncomfortably alien and puzzling to an average American audience.

Recent Works

Anouilh's most recent plays that are still un-collected find him characteristically exploring varying dramatic approaches to essentially familiar material.

In 1945 Anouilh published some fragments of an unfinished Orestes play; some twenty-five years later in *Tu étais si gentil quand tu étais petit* (1972) Anouilh was finally able to retell the story of the House of Atreus. His version of the legend involves a perform-ance of the Greek tragedy with musical accompani-ment. The orchestra that provides the musical and spoken commentary is, of course, the standard Anouilh café quartet. The musicians are petty, unpleasant, and selfish—for Anouilh, a precise image of everyday reality. And, of course, the deliberate juxtaposition of their world and that of classical tragedy is intentionally dis-concerting. The musicians see only the underside of the tragedy, and their comments reduce the legendary figures in scale and in dignity. But the sordid events comprising the lives of the musicians do not take on any compensatory grandeur. Everyone seems reduced to the lowest common denominator. The musicians even claim that they have lived out more "drama" than Aeschylus could ever have created: "The story of the house of Atreus does not impress me. Papa, even though he was a hunchback . . . did better than that." The bass-fiddle player is referring to her father who, when he caught his wife in bed with a dentist, killed wife and dentist, his three sons, the dog, and himself.

The final effect of this mixture of the heroic and the vulgar is unsatisfying. Many of the themes common to Anouilh's plays seem forced and false here. At times one has the impression that this play is merely a less effective reworking of earlier materials. Orestes' confrontation with his mother's lover, for example, is simply a replay of the Antigone-Creon debate, but thirty years after its initial statement the same vocabulary and the same arguments are not altogether convincing.

Monsieur Barnett (1974) is a short play Anouilh adapted from some of his unpublished material. As Monsieur Barnett, a successful businessman, sits in the barber chair, the comments of his sycophantic barber and manicurist provide some harsh and unpleasant comedy. This tone modulates into one of bitter melancholy when Monsieur Barnett, having suffered a fatal seizure, waits for death, consoled only by a rather immoral and cynical young shop attendant. The memories of the one love of his life, his pathetic desire not to die alone, the young girl who stays to sing to him the only popular song she knows, provide a brief but touching restatement of the terrifying solitude that confronts every one of Anouilh's heroes. In fact, the play is remarkable for expressing so many of Anouilh's favorite themes so sharply and concisely. The limited physical means available and the close proximity of actor and spectator in the *café-théâtre*—the equivalent of an Off-Broadway coffee-house theater—in which *Monsieur Barnett* was performed seem to have proved congenial restraints, removing some of the baroque elaboration of the later and for the most part less successful plays. Despite its brevity, *Monsieur Barnett* is a bitter, biting, and dense work.

In Anouilh's next play to be staged, *L'arrestation* (1975), the hero, arriving somewhat mysteriously at a once-elegant resort hotel, witnesses various scenes, which we gradually discover are moments of his own life. We see him as a child, often neglected by his mother, the pianist in the hotel orchestra, while she is with her lover. We see him as a young man, bored and uncomfortable with his young wife. And we see him with the vulgar and lascivious young woman for whom he deserts his wife and with whom he enters a life of crime, the two becoming, in fact, a French Bonnie and Clyde. In this play Anouilh departs from his usual pattern, for the abandoned child becomes not a playwright or director but a bank robber. The variation, however, is not particularly successful.

These scenes, we learn, are the final thoughts of the protagonist, who has been fatally injured in an automobile accident. With over-elaborate detail, one character explains that at the moment of death there is a final surge of blood to the brain, allowing the mind to continue to function after clinical death. As a plot device this proves weak and unconvincing. Although there are some remarkably effective moments, particularly when the mature man, the young criminal, and the abandoned child collectively conspire to take vengeance on the mother's lover, most of Anouilh's familiar elements, especially the shoddy orchestra, suffer from a serious lack of vitality.

Anouilh's very recent play *Le scénario* (1976) takes

place in a small inn outside of Paris, in which two writers are working on a film script. The time is August 1939. The two central characters, one young and idealistic, the other older and more pragmatic, are forced by their producer, a vulgar, uneducated Polish Jew, to turn their rather bittersweet love story into a commercial product. The drama, ending with the suicide of the older writer, is played against the growing threat of World War II. In fact, Hitler's voice on the radio is heard throughout the action, and war is declared before the final curtain.

The historical and political background is provocative and disconcerting. The contrast between the producer, presented in an almost stereotypically anti-Semitic fashion, and his aristocratic German assistant, who departs to recapture his honor by fighting for Hitler, is simplistic and raises unpleasant questions about Anouilh's politics. In other respects, *Le scénario* is dominated by conflicts and characters he has returned to again and again. Nor is it stylistically rewarding. Anouilh's language is uncharacteristically flat, and the over-long and somewhat repetitious speeches fail to create vivid characters.

Chers zoiseaux (1976) opened in Paris too late for more than a brief mention. Anouilh, continuing in a vein of bitter political commentary, has written a scathing attack on the whole spectrum of political commitment—right, left, and center—once again using a writer—this time of pot-boiler murder mysteries—as a central character.

"DOLEFUL MATTER
MERRILY SET DOWN"

In *The Winter's Tale,* one of the three
Shakespeare comedies Anouilh has translated, the clown
speaks of his preference for ballads that tell sad stories
in a pleasing and joyous way: "doleful matter merrily
set down." Such, indeed, is what Anouilh does in his
theater. In spite of his many attempts to pass himself
off as simply a popular entertainer, as a writer whose
sole aim is to please, Anouilh's plays seriously consider
disturbing moral and philosophical conflicts that neither
he nor we can resolve easily. His plays all ask the same
fundamental question: "How is one to live?" They bring
to mind Giraudoux's statement that "theater is the only
form of moral and artistic education of a nation."[1] As
an "educator," Anouilh is particularly appealing and
convincing because of his deep compassion and clear
vision. In addition, like his model, Molière, he keeps
firmly in mind the need to amuse the members of his
audience while he also assumes the deeper responsibility
of touching their souls.

Anouilh may choose to present his observations in the

guise of amusing fables, but one must not be deceived by their often pleasing surfaces; the vision underlying them is brutal and unpleasant:

> My theater is the Comtesse de Ségur [writer of children's fairy tales] alongside of the truth. If someday I ever write a book, I'll tell you what I really feel, and then you'll see that it won't be the Comtesse de Ségur.[2]

But in his theater, even at his most misanthropic, Anouilh offers a glimpse of an ideal, which, although faint or parodied, is not forgotten. In addition, Anouilh's belief in the possibility of man's survival in an inhospitable environment provides a note of optimism that lightens much of his writing. Anouilh the cynic cannot entirely suppress the frustrated idealist.

Anouilh's strength as a playwright, the reason for his eminence as a contemporary dramatist, comes from his ability to present in a large body of work and to an extremely wide audience a rich statement of a personal vision, a lucid yet entertaining exploration of themes that involve the anxieties and preoccupations of contemporary audiences. Although not as intellectual as some other twentieth-century French dramatists, Anouilh is unquestionably a master playmaker, one of the most accomplished craftsmen in modern French theater—indeed, in world theater. We respond deeply to the humanity of Anouilh's writing as we are dazzled by the brilliance of its form, for his work is both a synthesis of and a contribution to the most creative elements in modern drama.

NOTES

A Comic Misanthrope

1. Jean Anouilh, quoted in Ronald Hayman, *Playback*, London, Davis-Poynter, 1973, p. 24.
2. Ibid., p. 24.
3. Jean Anouilh, interviewed by Nicolas de Rabaudy, *Paris-Match*, Oct. 21, 1972, p. 86.
4. Ibid., p. 86.
5. Ibid., p. 89.
6. Jean Anouilh, quoted in Paul-Louis Mignon, "Le théâtre de A jusqu'à Z," *L'avant-scène*, Dec. 15, 1959, p. 6.
7. Anouilh, *Paris-Match* interview, p. 86.
8. Ibid., p. 88.
9. Jean Anouilh, quoted in Pol Vandromme, *Jean Anouilh: Un auteur et ses personnages*, Paris, Table Ronde, 1965, p. 176.
10. Ibid., p. 180.
11. Anouilh, *Paris-Match* interview, p. 89.
12. Jean Anouilh, "Hommage à Giraudoux," *Chronique de Paris*, Feb. 1944.
13. Jean Anouilh, "J'ai reçu un cadeau de Cocteau à 18 ans," *L'avant-scène*, Oct. 1–15, 1966, p. 26.

14. Jean Anouilh, "Cher Vitrac," *Le Figaro*, Oct. 1, 1962.
15. Anouilh, *Paris-Match* interview, p. 88.
16. Jean Anouilh, interviewed in *Opéra*, Feb. 14, 1951.
17. Anouilh, *Paris-Match* interview, p. 88.
18. Anouilh, "Cher Vitrac."
19. Jean Anouilh, "Présence de Molière," *Cahiers Renaud-Barrault*, May, 1959, p. 5.
20. Ibid., p. 5.
21. Ibid., p. 7.
22. Ibid., p. 7.
23. Jean Anouilh, *La répétition; ou, L'amour puni*, in *Pièces brillantes*, Paris, Table Ronde, 1951, p. 387.
24. Jean Anouilh, "Seul sur le plateau nu," *L'avant-scène*, Dec. 15, 1972, p. 8.
25. Anouilh, *Paris-Match* interview, p. 89.
26. Anouilh, quoted in Hayman, p. 28.

The Plays

1. Jean Anouilh, quoted in Ronald Hayman, *Playback*, London, Davis-Poynter, 1973, p. 24.
2. Jean Anouilh, quoted in Serge Radine, *Anouilh, Lenormand, Salacrou: Trois dramaturges à la recherche de leur vérité*, Geneva, Trois Collines, 1951, p. 43.
3. Jean-Paul Sartre, "Forgers of Myths," *Theatre Arts*, June, 1946, p. 331.
4. Jean Giraudoux, *Paris Impromptu, Tulane Drama Review*, Summer, 1959, p. 109.
5. Jean Anouilh, "*La valse des toréadors*? Que voilà une bonne pièce," *Le Figaro*, Jan. 23, 1952.
6. Jean Anouilh, "Des ciseaux de papa au 'Sabre de mon père,'" *Opéra*, March 7, 1951.
7. Jean Anouilh, "Une inexplicable joie," *L'avant-scène*, Oct. 15, 1964, p. 9.
8. Jean Anouilh, "Jean Anouilh présente *Becket*," *L'avant-scène*, Feb. 15–March 1, 1963, p. 10.
9. Jean Anouilh, "Jean Anouilh présente *La foire d'empoigne*," *L'avant-scène*, Feb. 15–March 1, 1963, p. 56.
10. Jean Anouilh, "Seul sur le plateau nu," *L'avant-scène*, Dec. 15, 1972, p. 8.

"Doleful Matter Merrily Set Down"

1. Jean Giraudoux, "Discours sur le théâtre," *Littérature*, Paris, Grasset, 1941, p. 233.
2. Jean Anouilh, interviewed by Nicolas de Rabaudy, *Paris-Match*, Oct. 21, 1972, p. 86.

BIBLIOGRAPHY

I. Plays of Jean Anouilh

L'alouette [The Lark]
> Paris, Table Ronde, 1953; in *Pièces costumées*.
> *The Lark*, tr. Christopher Fry. New York, Oxford University Press, 1956.
> *The Lark*, tr. Lillian Hellman. New York, Random House, 1956; in *Five Plays*, Vol II, New York, Hill and Wang, 1959.

Antigone [Antigone]
> Paris, Table Ronde, 1944; in *Nouvelles pièces noires*.
> *Antigone*, tr. Lewis Galantière. New York, Random House, 1946; in *Five Plays*, Vol. I, New York, Hill and Wang, 1958.

Ardèle; ou, La marguerite [Ardele; or, The Daisy]
> Paris, Table Ronde, 1949; in *Pièces grinçantes*.
> *Ardèle*, tr. Lucienne Hill. London, Methuen, 1951; in *Five Plays*, Vol. II, New York, Hill and Wang, 1959.

L'arrestation [The Arrest]
> Paris, Table Ronde, 1975.

Le bal des voleurs [The Thieves' Ball]
> Paris, Fayard, 1938; in *Pièces roses*.
> *Thieves' Carnival*, tr. Lucienne Hill. New York,

Samuel French, 1956; in *Seven Plays*, Vol III, New York, Hill and Wang, 1967.

Becket; ou, L'honneur de Dieu [Becket; or, God's Honor]
Paris, Table Ronde, 1959; in *Pièces costumées.*
Becket, tr. Lucienne Hill. New York, Coward-McCann, 1960.

Le boulanger, la boulangère et le petit mitron [The Baker, The Baker's Wife, and the Little Baker Boy]
Paris, Table Ronde, 1968; in *Nouvelles pièces grinçantes.*

Cécile; ou, L'école des pères [Cecile; or, The School for Fathers]
In *Pièces brillantes.*
Cecile, tr. Luce and Arthur Klein. In *Seven Plays*, Vol III, New York, Hill and Wang, 1967.

Cher Antoine; ou, L'amour raté [Dear Antoine; or, Love's Failure]
Paris, Table Ronde, 1969; in *Pièces baroques.*
Dear Antoine, tr. Lucienne Hill. New York, Hill and Wang, 1971.

Colombe [Colombe]
In *Pièces brillantes.*
Mademoiselle Colombe, tr. Louis Kronenberger. New York, Coward-McCann, 1954; *Five Plays*, Vol II, Hill and Wang, 1959.

Le directeur de l'Opéra [The Director of the Opera]
Paris, Table Ronde, 1972; in *Pièces baroques.*

Episode de la vie d'un auteur [Episode in the Life of an Author]
In *Cahiers Renaud-Barrault*, May, 1959.
Episode in the Life of an Author, tr. Miriam John. In *Seven Plays*, Vol. III, New York, Hill and Wang, 1967.

Eurydice [Eurydice]
In *Pièces noires.*
Legend of Lovers, tr. Kitty Black. New York, Coward-McCann, 1952; in *Five Plays*, Vol. I, New York, Hill and Wang, 1958.

La foire d'empoigne [Catch as Catch Can]
In *Pièces costumées.*
Catch as Catch Can, tr. Lucienne Hill. In *Seven Plays*, Vol. III, New York, Hill and Wang, 1967.

La grotte [The Cave]
> Paris, Table Ronde, 1961; in *Nouvelles pièces grinçantes*.
> *The Cavern*, tr. Lucienne Hill. New York, Hill and Wang, 1966.

L'hermine [The Ermine]
> Paris, Fayard, 1934; in *Pièces noires*.
> *The Ermine*, tr. Miriam John. In *Five Plays*, Vol. I, New York, Hill and Wang, 1958.

Humulus le muet [Humulus the Mute]
> In *Pièces roses*.

L'hurluberlu; ou, Le réactionnaire amoureux [The Scatterbrain; or, The Reactionary in Love]
> Paris, Table Ronde, 1959; in *Nouvelles Pièces grinçantes*.
> *The Fighting Cock*, tr. Lucienne Hill. New York, Hill and Wang, 1960.

L'invitation au château [The Invitation to the Chateau]
> Paris, Table Ronde, 1948; in *Pièces brillantes.*
> *Ring Round the Moon*, tr. Christopher Fry. New York, Oxford University Press, 1950.

Jézabel [Jezabel]
> In *Nouvelles pièces noires*.

Léocadia [Léocadia]
> In *Pièces roses.*
> *Time Remembered*, tr. Patricia Moyes. New York, Coward-McCann, 1958; in *Five Plays*, Vol. II, New York, Hill and Wang, 1959.

Médée [Medea]
> In *Nouvelles pièces noires.*
> *Medea*, tr. Luce and Arthur Klein. In Eric Bentley, ed., *The Modern Theater*, Vol. V, New York, Doubleday, 1957; in *Seven Plays*, Vol. III, New York, Hill and Wang, 1967.

Monsieur Barnett [Mr. Barnett]
> In *L'avant-scène*, March 1, 1965.

Ne réveillez pas Madame [Don't Awaken Madame]
> Paris, Table Ronde, 1970; in *Pièces baroques*.

Nouvelles pièces grinçantes
> *L'Hurluberlu; ou, Le réactionnaire amoureux, La grotte, L'orchestre, Le boulanger, la boulangère et le*

petit mitron, Les poissons rouges; ou, Mon père, ce héros.
Paris, Table Ronde, 1970.
Nouvelles pièces noires
Jézabel, Antigone, Roméo et Jeannette, Médée.
Paris, Table Ronde, 1946.
L'orchestre [The Orchestra]
In Nouvelles pièces grinçantes.
The Orchestra, tr. Miriam John. In Seven Plays, Vol. III, New York, Hill and Wang, 1967.
Oreste [Orestes]
In Robert de Luppé, Jean Anouilh. Paris, Éditions Universitaires, 1959.
Ornifle; ou, Le courant d'air [Ornifle; or, The Draft]
Paris, Table Ronde, 1956; in Pièces grinçantes.
Ornifle, tr. Lucienne Hill. New York, Hill and Wang, 1970.
Pauvre Bitos; ou, Le dîner de têtes [Poor Bitos; or, The Masquerade Dinner Party]
In Pièces grinçantes.
Poor Bitos, tr. Lucienne Hill. New York, Coward-McCann, 1964.
La petite Molière [Moliere's Young Wife]
In L'avant-scène, Dec. 15, 1959.
Pièces baroques
Cher Antoine; ou, L'amour raté, Ne réveillez pas madame, Le directeur de l'Opéra.
Paris, Table Ronde, 1974.
Pièces brillantes
L'invitation au château, Colombe, La répétition; ou, L'amour puni, Cécile; ou, L'école des pères.
Paris, Table Ronde, 1951.
Pièces costumées
L'alouette, Becket; ou, L'honneur de Dieu, La foire d'empoigne.
Paris, Table Ronde, 1960.
Pièces grinçantes
Ardèle; ou, La marguerite, La valse des toréadors, Ornifle; ou, Le courant d'air, Pauvre Bitos; ou, Le dîner de têtes.
Paris, Table Ronde, 1956.

Pièces noires
> *L'hermine, La sauvage, Le voyageur sans bagage, Eurydice.*
> Paris, Ed. Balzac, 1942.

Pièces roses
> *Humulus le muet, Le bal des voleurs, Le rendez-vous de Senlis, Léocadia.*
> Paris, Ed. Balzac, 1942.

Les poissons rouges; ou, Mon père, ce héros [The Goldfish; or My Father, the Hero]
> Paris, Table Ronde, 1970; in *Nouvelles pièces grinçantes.*

Le rendez-vous de Senlis [Rendez-vous at Senlis]
> In *Piéces roses.*
> *Dinner with the Family,* tr. Edward Owen Marsh. London, Methuen, 1958.

La répétition; ou, L'amour puni [The Rehearsal; or, Love Punished]
> Genève, La Palatine, 1950; in *Pièces brillantes.*
> *The Rehearsal,* tr. Pamela Hansford Johnson and Kitty Black. New York, Coward-McCann, 1962; in *Five Plays,* Vol. I, New York, Hill and Wang, 1958.

Roméo et Jeannette [Romeo and Jeannette]
> In *Nouvelles pièces noires.*
> *Romeo and Jeannette,* tr. Miriam John. In *Five Plays,* Vol. I, New York, Hill and Wang, 1958.

La sauvage [The Untamed Girl]
> Paris, Fayard, 1938; in *Pièces noires.*
> *Restless Heart,* tr. Lucienne Hill. London, Methuen, 1957; in *Five Plays,* Vol. II, New York, Hill and Wang, 1959.

Le scénario [The Script]
> Paris, Table Ronde, 1976.

Le songe du critique [The Critic's Dream]
> In *L'avant-scène,* May 15, 1961.

Tu étais si gentil quand tu étais petit [You Used to Be So Nice when You Were Little]
> Paris, Table Ronde, 1972.

La valse des toréadors [The Waltz of the Toreadors]
> Paris, Table Ronde, 1952; in *Pièces grinçantes.*
> *Waltz of the Toreadors,* tr. Lucienne Hill. New York, Coward-McCann, 1957.

Le voyageur sans bagage [Traveler without Luggage]
In *L'illustration*, April 10, 1937; in *Pièces noires. Traveler Without Luggage*, tr. John Whiting. London, Methuen, 1959; in *Seven Plays*, Vol. III, New York, Hill and Wang, 1967.
Y *avait un prisonnier* [There Once Was a Prisoner]
In *L'illustration*, May 18, 1935.

II. Articles by Jean Anouilh *(in chronological order)*

"Monsieur Dullin," Program of the Compagnie des Quatre Saisons de Paris, Théâtre de l'Atelier, 1940.
"Mon cher Pitoëff," *Aujourd'hui*, Sept. 11, 1948.
"Propos déplacés," *La gerbe*, Nov. 14, 1940.
"Hommage à Giraudoux," *Chronique de Paris*, Feb., 1944.
"Lettre," in Hubert Gignoux, *Jean Anouilh*, Paris, Temps Présent, 1946.
"Hommage à Georges Pitoëff," *Opéra*, May 4, 1949.
"Denis Malclès," Program for *La répétition*, Compagnie Renaud-Barrault, 1950.
"Des ciseaux de papa au 'Sabre de mon père,' " *Opéra*, March 7, 1951.
"Ludmilla Pitoëff," *Opéra*, Sept. 9, 1951.
"*La valse des toréadors*? Que voilà une bonne pièce," *Le Figaro*, Jan. 23, 1952.
"*Godot* ou le sketch des *Pensées* de Pascal traité par les Fratellini," *Arts*, Feb. 27, 1953.
"Lettre à une jeune fille qui veut faire du théâtre," *Elle*, Jan. 21, 1955.
"La mort d'une troupe," *Arts*, Oct. 19, 1955.
"Du chapitre des chaises," *Le Figaro*, April 23, 1956.
"Lettre d'un vieux crocodile à un jeune mousquetaire," *Arts*, May 1, 1957.
"Présence de Molière," Program of the Comédie Française, Jan. 15, 1959. Reprinted in *Cahiers Renaud-Barrault*, May, 1959.
"Il y a dix ans mourait Charles Dullin," *Le Figaro*, Dec. 12, 1959.
"*Becket* by Chance," *The New York Times*, Oct. 2, 1960.
"Cher Vitrac," *Le Figaro*, Oct. 1, 1962.

"Dans mon trou de souffleur pour la première fois j'au eu peur au théâtre," *Paris-Match*, Oct. 20, 1962.
Notes on *Becket* and *La foire d'empoigne*, in *L'avant-scène*, Feb. 15–March 1, 1963.
"Le bon pain," *Le Figaro*, June 9, 1960.
"Mystère de Jeanne," *L'avant-scène*, Oct. 15, 1964.
"Une inexplicable joie," *L'avant-scène*, Oct. 15, 1964.
"Pour un instant de théâtre," *Le Figaro*, Sept. 29, 1966.
"J'ai reçu un cadeau de Cocteau à 18 ans," *L'avant-scène*, Oct. 1–15, 1966.
"Mon père ce héros," *L'avant-scène*, Sept. 1, 1971.
"Avertissement prudent," *L'avant-scène*, July 15, 1972.
Interview by Nicolas de Rabaudy, *Paris-Match*, Oct. 21, 1972.
"Faire rire," *L'avant-scène*, May 15, 1974.

III. Selected Criticism

Albérès, René-Marill, *La révolte des écrivains d'aujourd'hui*, Paris, Corrêa, 1949.
Archer, Marguerite, *Anouilh*, New York, Columbia University Press, 1971.
Bishop, Thomas, *Pirandello and the French Theater*, New York, New York University Press, 1960.
Borgal, Clément, *Anouilh: La peine de vivre*, Paris, Éditions du Centurion, 1966.
Chiari, Joseph, *The Contemporary French Theatre: The Flight from Naturalism*, London, Rockliff, 1958.
Della Fazia, Alba, *Jean Anouilh*, New York, Twayne, 1969.
Didier, Jean, *À la rencontre de Jean Anouilh*, Brussels, La Sixaine, 1946.
Fowlie, Wallace, *Dionysus in Paris: A Guide to French Contemporary Theater*, New York, Meridian, 1959.
Gignoux, Hubert, *Jean Anouilh*, Paris, Temps Présent, 1946.
Ginestier, Paul, *Anouilh*, Paris, Éditions Seghers, 1969.
Grossvogel, David I., *The Self-conscious Stage in Modern French Theater*, New York, Columbia University Press, 1958.
Guicharnaud, Jacques, *Modern French Theater from Giraudoux to Beckett*, New Haven, Conn., Yale University Press, 1961.

Harvey, John, *Anouilh: A Study in Theatrics*, New Haven, Conn., Yale University Press, 1964.

Hobson, Harold, *The French Theatre of Today: An English View*, London, Harrap, 1953.

Jolivet, P., *Le théâtre de Jean Anouilh*, Paris, Michel Briant, 1963.

Lasalle, Jean-Pierre, *Jean Anouilh; ou, La vaine révolte*, Rodez, France, Éditions Subervie, 1958.

Luppé, Robert de, *Jean Anouilh*, Paris, Éditions Universitaires, 1959.

Marsh, Edward Owen, *Jean Anouilh: Poet of Pierrot and Pantaloon*, London, W. H. Allen, 1953.

Mury, G., *Anouilh devant l'action; ou, La prison sans barreaux*, Paris, Seghers, 1946.

Pronko, Leonard Cabell, *The World of Jean Anouilh*, Berkeley, University of California Press, 1961.

Radine, Serge, *Anouilh, Lenormand, Salacrou: Trois dramaturges à la recherche de leur vérité*, Geneva, Trois Collines, 1951.

Thody, P., *Anouilh*, Edinburgh, Oliver and Boyd, 1968.

Vandromme, Pol, *Jean Anouilh: Un auteur et ses personnages*, Paris, Table Ronde, 1965.

INDEX